life
After Debt

Is Personal Bankruptcy
Your Best Solution?

Frank S. Kisluk, BA, CA, CIP, CFE
Trustee in Bankruptcy

Doubleday Canada Limited

Canadian Cataloguing in Publication Data

Kisluk, Frank
   Life after debt: is personal bankruptcy your best solution?

Rev. & updated.
ISBN 0-385-25873-9

1. Bankruptcy – Canada.   2. Finance, Personal – Canada.
I. Title.

HG3769.C34K57 1999   332.7'5'0971   C98-932862-7

Cover design by Designmode Communications Inc.
Text design by Heidy Lawrance Associates
Printed and bound in Canada

Published in Canada by
Doubleday Canada Limited
105 Bond Street
Toronto, Ontario
M5B 1Y3

TRAN 10 9 8 7 6 5 4 3 2 1

CONTENTS

ACKNOWLEDGEMENTS

This book reflects more than twenty years of managing a busy professional insolvency practice that has often competed with my family for my time and attention. Throughout those years I have always been supported and encouraged in these endeavours by my wife, Marilyn, and my daughter, Michelle. Without their support, this book and all it represents would not have happened.

J. Murray Ferron, Registrar in Bankruptcy in the Ontario Court of Justice, kindly read an early manuscript and gave me the encouragement and support to finish the book. The Honourable Mr. Justice James M. Farley of the Ontario Court of Justice reviewed a later manuscript and provided his insights and suggestions which I have incorporated into this final version. I thank both of them for their generous assistance.

And thank you to the countless individuals who, over the years, have passed through my office and trustingly shared their feelings with me while facing their financial crises. I have tried to respond to their concerns and, hopefully, to the concerns of others facing similar financial problems.

AUTHOR'S NOTE

Bankruptcy is one of the least understood processes in our legal system. Even though tens of thousands of individuals file for bankruptcy in Canada every year, the process is a private affair, and not the subject of public articles and explanations. Usually the person who files for bankruptcy deals only with his or her creditors, unless there are unusual matters which must be brought before a court. That is why most of the things that you have heard about bankruptcy were probably told to you by people who had filed for bankruptcy themselves. Unfortunately, their stories are told from their own very personal perspective and do not always apply to other people's situations.

Life After Debt explains how the Canadian personal bankruptcy system really works. You will be taken through the process from the very beginning, from the moment you are wondering how you will deal with your personal debt and your first meeting with a trustee in bankruptcy. Together, we will look at the procedures with which a trustee can help you, through the filing, the creditors' meeting and the period during which you are in bankruptcy. We will then follow the process through to your discharge from bankruptcy and consider what you can expect from the future. We'll even review a plan to rebuild your credit. And, along the way, we'll look at other options that you can follow on your own or with a trustee's help.

Life After Debt will:

- help you understand what bankruptcy and proposals are all about;
- answer many of your questions and concerns;
- allow you to make an informed decision about whether bankruptcy or a proposal is a possible solution to your personal financial problems.

If you are determined to escape the debt trap and take back control of your finances from your creditors, you must first understand your rights and your options. As we review them together you will see that there are a number of steps that you can take, on your own, to regain financial control. These are covered in Chapter 2, "Recognizing a Debt Problem and Getting Out of It".

On the other hand, if you are unable to rearrange your affairs using the approaches suggested, there is still relief for the debtor who genuinely cannot pay his or her bills. In fact, there must be relief from debt because, otherwise, the penalty for uncontrolled debt would be continuing to live in a state of financial inertia – no one would take any risks and then no one could succeed. The legal processes of the Bankruptcy and Insolvency Act are therefore available to allow an individual to claim a fresh start in life. Together, we'll look at these procedures in plain nontechnical terms.

And finally, I want to remove the mystery associated with qualifying for credit. I will share with you some proven steps that anyone can take to rebuild his or her personal credit rating, whether or not you have filed for bankruptcy protection.

I hope you will then have the confidence to seize control of your financial life.

CAUTION

Bankruptcy is a legal process. How your trustee and creditors respond to your bankruptcy and how it affects you are determined by both written law (statute) and court decisions (common law). The law and rules change as the courts issue new decisions and the government changes policy. Therefore this book can only reflect the situation as it presently exists. Since this book explains only the most important issues, you should not make any decision based on this material without also consulting a professional advisor (accountant, lawyer or trustee).

INTRODUCTION

**PERSONAL BANKRUPTCIES AND
PROPOSALS FILED IN CANADA**
1966 to 1998

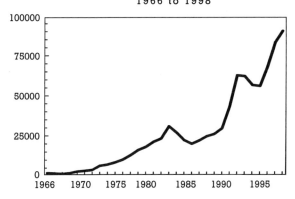

The number of personal bankruptcies filed in Canada has grown from 1,900 in 1966 to a projected 95,000 in 1999, as shown on the above chart. The experience of personal bankruptcy continues to be a constant fixture in our society. Even the recessions of 1982 and 1992 appear, on this chart, to be merely unusual events that have only a short-term dampening effect on the growing levels of personal bankruptcies.

To understand this growth in bankruptcies, one must

1

examine the dramatic change in the structure of our economic system, particularly over the past 20 years. During that period credit has become commonplace. This change is reflected in an outpouring of credit cards from both financial institutions and merchants. For example, in 1977 there were 8.2 million active Canadian MasterCard and Visa credit cards. Today there are more than 32 million. In the same period, debt carried on those cards rose from $1.4 billion to over $20 billion. It is likely that credit cards will continue to flood our system and the potential for overextension of credit and bankruptcy will remain high.

In my professional practice as a trustee in bankruptcy over the past 22 years, I have observed the increasing fragility of personal financial security as people have accumulated staggering and unprecedented levels of credit card debt. That debt carries with it a required minimum monthly payment that quickly becomes a financial albatross, ever present and ever demanding. Under these circumstances a financial crisis arises when some unplanned event intervenes, such as the loss of a family's second income, a major illness or even an unexpected expense, such as a car repair. With no financial cushion, many individuals suddenly find themselves in financial chaos. Unaware of the rights and options available to them, people often become resigned to living in a state of constant financial stress, afraid and feeling trapped.

1

——

Relieving Stress
and Gaining Control
of Your Finances

The expression "money isn't everything!" is certainly true. Our lives contain many things that are ultimately more important to us than money itself. Most of us want, above all, to enjoy our relationships with our spouses, our children and our friends. We want a job that gives us personal satisfaction and a feeling of accomplishment. Or we might want to be a part of a larger group or club, sharing and enjoying common interests.

Money may not be everything but it plays such an important role in our lives that when our finances are not under control, all other facets of our lives are negatively affected.

As your debts grow and your creditors begin to demand repayment, you must use your limited, and usually unchangeable income to meet more and more demands for repayment. Add to this the need to allocate money for day-to-day living costs and unplanned expenses, the pressures that accumulate can become overwhelming.

As you face increasing demands for repayment, the stress that you experience in your personal relationships continues to grow and there is less and less room to maneuver. Unfortunately, as I have too often seen in these situations, separation, divorce and lost friendships are often the result of financial stress. Stress can also affect your health. When financial pressure cannot be relieved, the resultant stress often culminates in physical illnesses and even serious ailments.

Now, imagine a hot water boiler or a pressure cooker, as it heats up. When the internal pressure increases to a certain level, the pressure must be released or the container will explode. Opening a valve and releasing the steam pressure allows the vessel to return to a state where it can continue to perform efficiently. If your personal financial pressure cannot be relieved by one or more of the approaches discussed in Chapter 2, filing for bankruptcy may be the valve that restores balance to your life. By ending your debts and the pressure from creditors, bankruptcy allows you the opportunity to regain control of your life, restore your personal dignity and enjoy peace of mind.

FEAR IS NOT A FOUR-LETTER WORD

Insolvency and bankruptcy and our personal obligations to our creditors, are kept in balance by our fear of the unknown, our fear of failure and our fear of risk. But it is important to understand that just as those fears can have a positive effect on how we interact in our economic environment, they can also become negative factors that hold us back from getting ahead with our lives.

FEAR OF THE UNKNOWN

Fear of the unknown can be an obstacle that prevents us from taking new steps or making decisions that could allow us to escape a situation. Sometimes we imagine the consequences of taking certain steps, assuming the worst possible outcomes. And often, we begin to believe that those assumptions are factual and real.

For example, if a creditor threatens to sue your spouse for your debt, you might conclude that because you are married, your debts are also the responsibility of your spouse. However, in law, unless the loan was made to both of you, or your spouse guaranteed your loan, it is only in extraordinary circumstances that your spouse would have any liability. Yet that threat, combined with a story of someone you know whose spouse had to pay a debt, may be the link that creates "fact" from fear.

FEAR OF FAILURE

Another fear that blocks action is our fear of acknowledging failure. There is a giant step between failing and openly admitting that we have failed. In a world filled with marketing for success, we are always reminded that the goal in life is success. Magazines, television programs, seminars, advertisements, books and special mail offers, all are selling success. No wonder we look in the mirror and feel disappointed when comparing our personal condition with the image being sold to us. We forget that we are trying to live up to a "marketing" image.

So it is natural to become afraid. Afraid to admit that, apparently, unlike the rest of the world, we have failed while everyone else appears to have succeeded. The truth is that many people fail and then go on to succeed.

FEAR OF RISK

In order to succeed, we take risks. We risk our money in an investment, our time in a new project or our livelihood by working for a single employer and depending on that employer's success to give us a secure income. Yet sometimes those risks do not result in success. Sometimes we have setbacks. That does not mean that we must hide from risk. Every new situation in our lives carries some level of risk.

OVERCOMING FEAR

Fear immobilizes and prevents us from making decisions and taking steps which could free us from the trap of debt. To overcome that fear and take control of our financial lives, we must eliminate the unknown. We must understand the nature of our perceived failure and must have enough facts before us to be able to assess any risk associated with confronting our problems.

2

Recognizing a
Debt Problem and
Getting Out of It

The first step toward solving any problem is recognizing its symptoms. You have, or will have, a debt problem if:

- you continually exceed your spending limit or you use your credit cards as a necessity rather than a convenience;
- you are always borrowing money from friends and co-workers to make it from one payday to the next;
- your wages have been garnisheed to pay for out-standing debts;
- you pay only interest or service charges monthly and do not reduce your total debt over many months;
- creditors and collection agencies harass you for payment, threaten to sue or repossess the goods you bought on credit; and

- utility companies cut off service because your bills have gone unpaid.

(reproduced from "Dealing with Debt: A Consumer's Guide," Industry Canada, Bankruptcy Division)

If you can identify with any of the above, you are not in full control of your financial affairs. The first step to taking control is to get information about the options available to you.

As a trustee in bankruptcy for the past 20 years, I have met with thousands of people, helping them to confront their debt problems and take control of their financial lives. Having a financial problem does not automatically lead to personal bankruptcy. Most people have the ability to change their financial situation and to take control of their financial lives, if they confront their problems at an early stage. The following is a summary of approaches available to you in confronting and overcoming the pressures of debt.

1. Lock Your Cards In A Safety Deposit Box

The simplest way to stop increasing your debt is to stop using your credit cards. Take every one out of your purse or wallet and lock them away! In fact, it might be best to destroy them. If this idea scares you, that is all the more reason to make this commitment up front. Otherwise, any other efforts will be futile. This is your first step on the road to financial recovery; there is no place for credit cards in any serious program to regain control of your finances.

2. The Simplest Way Out Of Debt – Pay It

If you are ever to stop the debt cycle, you must get rid of the debt. Too often, because a creditor requires only a minimum payment each month on the outstanding balance, you will find yourself making only that payment. You might then feel comfortable spending your remaining money on yourself.

Consider increasing the monthly payments required by ten percent. Instead of the $200 required as payment, begin paying $220 every month. Investment advisors talk of compound interest's amazing ability to increase your savings, if you would only put aside a small amount every month. The same argument holds true for reducing your debts. A modest increase in your monthly payments on your credit cards and loans will have them fully paid in a markedly shorter time.

3. Debt Consolidation

If you are committed to making monthly payments on several debts and the total of those payments has become too large to handle, consider borrowing the total amount of

11

those debts from a new lender, preferably a bank at competitive rates. This would allow you to pay off all of the old debts with a single reduced monthly payment on the one new consolidated loan. If you can do this, you will satisfy all of your creditors and maintain your credit rating.

4. Pay The Most Expensive Debt First

Review your debts and list them according to the interest rate being charged – from highest to lowest rate. When you allocate your increased monthly minimum payments, apply the increase first to the most expensive debt. In this way, you will minimize the outflow of interest money and pay off the principal part of the debt faster.

5. Communicating And Negotiating With Your Creditors

Always keep in touch with your creditors. Imagine how you would feel if someone owed you money, didn't pay you, and didn't return your phone calls or respond to your letters. It is critical that you advise your creditors that you are having a problem; share your situation with them; and tell them what you are doing to fix the situation. Honest communication is the most important factor in gaining your creditors' support and assistance.

Some of the kinds of assistance which might be available from your creditors are:

- A reduced monthly payment.
- A period of time during which you will not make payments.
- Reduction or elimination of interest charges. Possibly all future payments could be applied entirely to the reduction of the outstanding principal balance.
- An absolute reduction in the total amount of the debt.

In fact, this restructuring of debt could take any form mutually agreed upon between you and your creditors. Once you have come to an agreement with your creditors, document the new arrangements. It is best to have a separate written agreement with each creditor, stating the amount of the debt, the rate of interest (if any) to be charged and the new terms of repayment.

Clearly, this form of restructuring is easier to accomplish if there are only a few creditors involved. Expect your creditors to demand equal treatment. If you cannot get everyone to agree to the revised debt structure, you may not be able to obtain a commitment from any of your creditors. After all, why should one creditor agree to accommodate you while other creditors are receiving full payment?

When there are too many creditors involved, and making an informal arrangement is impractical, another option to consider is filing a formal proposal to creditors under

13

the Bankruptcy & Insolvency Act. That approach will be dealt with more fully later in the book.

6. Credit Counselling Services

Most metropolitan centers in Canada have a credit counselling service available to help you manage your debt. These agencies are funded by the government and credit grantors (e.g., MasterCard, Visa). A user fee is usually charged to clients, based on their ability to pay.

These agencies will assist you in dealing with your creditors and will attempt to negotiate a repayment plan that satisfies both you and your creditors. If you were successful in this restructuring, you would then make one monthly payment to the credit counselling agency which would distribute the money to your creditors.

3

Bankruptcy –
A Brief History

Imagine a sunny day in Genoa, Italy, around the year 1500. In order to finance the growing trade with distant cities, some merchants have invested their money to buy ships and finance journeys to far-off countries, to trade Italian olive oil and other goods for merchandise to be sold in Genoa. The investors meet in a large room near the docks, each seated at a bench awaiting news of his ship's fate. In those days, there was always a great danger that a ship could be lost at sea. A messenger enters with news that a ship has been reported lost. Along with the ship, the merchant has lost all of his money invested in that journey. He stands up at his bench ("banca") and publicly acknowledges his financial failure by breaking the bench ("rupta"). And so we have the term "banca rupta" or "bankrupt", meaning financial failure.

If you were living in England during the time of Charles Dickens and could not pay your debts, all of your family assets could be seized by your creditors and you might find yourself in debtors' prison. There would be no chance of release from prison until all of your debts were paid. Obviously this system never allowed debtors to regain freedom because, while in jail, they had no chance to earn money to repay their creditors.

Today we have outlawed that approach. In Canada, the Bankruptcy Act of 1918 provided for an orderly settling of affairs and an opportunity for the bankrupt person to return to the economy as a productive individual.

Even though the original Bankruptcy Act was written in this century, it reflected the fact that financial failure was generally associated with businesses. Therefore, the emphasis remained on how to deal with a failed business and its creditors. Consumer debtors were only addressed as a secondary area of concern.

It was not until 1992, when Canada's Bankruptcy Act was changed significantly, and renamed the Bankruptcy and Insolvency Act, that a system was introduced to comprehensively address the specific concerns of the consumer debtor – the individual. These recent changes became necessary because of the significant increase in consumer credit through such innovations as credit cards and leasing contracts. The Bankruptcy and Insolvency Act continues to be fine-tuned through ongoing amendments, the most recent having been passed in 1997 and 1998.

As more of our spending is managed through credit, there are more opportunities for an individual's finances to become overextended. As a result, some unforseen event such as major illness or loss of employment can trigger a rush of creditors demanding payment. Although some may have prepared for such a catastrophe by setting aside money for that "rainy day," many of us are still caught without the proverbial umbrella in place.

Since our 20th-century economic system has been built on, and relies on, credit, the escape valve of personal bankruptcy has become necessary. The new Bankruptcy and Insolvency Act recognizes that bankruptcy is an integral part of this economic system.

4
—

The Bankruptcy and Insolvency Act – Bankruptcy Defined

The Canadian statute that deals with financial insolvency is the Bankruptcy and Insolvency Act (BIA). The BIA is a federal statute and applies to all parts of Canada and was passed to help individuals or companies who cannot pay debts when due.

As it applies to individuals, bankruptcy assists the honest debtor who gets into financial difficulties and is unable to meet his or her financial obligations. The purpose of the BIA is to provide a legal framework within which debtors and creditors can work together, coming to a final and honest accounting, after which the debtor will be allowed to proceed unburdened by the financial problems of the past.

A very important feature of Canadian personal bankruptcy legislation is its strong emphasis on the financial rehabilitation of the bankrupt individual. For the honest debtor – the person who has fallen on hard times, lost a job, suffered a severe illness or some other unexpected hardship or has simply lost control of his or her personal finances – the Bankruptcy and Insolvency Act provides a positive and helpful route to recovery.

It is very important to make clear the distinction between two terms: *insolvency* and *bankruptcy*.

In general terms, insolvency means the inability to pay your bills when they are due. The BIA defines an *insolvent person* as

> *a person who is not bankrupt and who resides or carries on business in Canada, whose liabilities to creditors ... amount to [at least] one thousand dollars, and ... who is for any reason unable to meet his obligations as they generally become due ...*

The actual legal definition contains other situations which would demonstrate insolvency, but this definition applies in most instances.

Bankruptcy, on the other hand, is a specific legal term. The technical term for filing bankruptcy is to *assign* oneself into bankruptcy. Hence, the BIA defines a bankrupt person, or *bankrupt*, as

> *a person who has made an assignment....*

Bankruptcy is the process by which one *assigns* to a trustee all of one's assets for the general benefit of his or her creditors. The trustee then, with certain important exceptions, converts those assets into cash (known as realizing on them) and distributes the proceeds to the creditors. In return, the creditors no longer have any legal claim against the individual for the part of the debt that the trustee was unable to satisfy.

It is important to keep this distinction in mind when discussing bankruptcy. You are not bankrupt until you have signed a set of papers and *assigned* yourself into bankruptcy through a trustee. Many people are *insolvent* because they cannot keep up with the required payments to their creditors. Insolvent persons become bankrupt when they assign themselves into bankruptcy.

You may have heard of a creditor threatening to *petition* someone into bankruptcy. This is a second way that a person can become bankrupt. The creditor must file a document with the court, asking or *petitioning* the court to declare that a debtor (the person owing the debt) be placed in bankruptcy. The creditor must satisfy the court that the debtor has committed an *act of bankruptcy*, the most common one being *unable to meet his or her obligations as they generally fall due.* If the court decides that the individual should be declared bankrupt, it will issue a *receiving order* that appoints a trustee who will take possession of the debtor's assets and who will deal with them as required under the BIA. (This will be discussed in greater detail in Chapter 10).

The third and only other way a person can become bankrupt is to have his or her *proposal* to creditors under the BIA turned down by them. (This will be more fully explained in Chapter 11.)

In the vast majority of cases, people become bankrupt only when they choose to do so (i.e., when they file an assignment).

5

Personal Bankruptcy: The Players and the Process

Let's take a look at the cast of characters with whom you will deal if you file under the BIA.

THE TRUSTEE IN BANKRUPTCY

You must file bankruptcy through a trustee in bankruptcy. A trustee is licensed by the superintendent of bankruptcy and, in most cases, is a chartered accountant who has specialized in the area of bankruptcy, met certain experience requirements, and has passed both written and oral examinations.

Once your bankruptcy is filed, the trustee's role is to represent all of your creditors and to ensure that the administration of your bankruptcy estate is conducted with regard to both your rights as the bankrupt and the rights

---

of your creditors. Although this may sound as if the trustee has a conflict of interest, you will find that the trustee will openly explain your rights and those of your creditors before you file the bankruptcy.

THE SUPERINTENDENT OF BANKRUPTCY

Although there is one person in Ottawa who has this title, the bankruptcy system is administered through many offices across the country. Each is an office of Industry Canada, Bankruptcy Division, and is under the day-to-day administration of an assistant superintendent of bankruptcy. Therefore, when a trustee files an assignment in bankruptcy on behalf of an individual, the documents are filed with the superintendent in the office in the locale of the debtor.

OFFICIAL RECEIVER

The actual management of files in the bankruptcy offices is conducted by individuals who are called official receivers. In most personal bankruptcy administrations, bankrupts do not deal with the official receivers.

BEGINNING THE BANKRUPTCY PROCESS
1. Choosing A Trustee

When choosing a trustee, as is the case with choosing any professional such as a doctor, accountant or lawyer, you should first consider asking someone for a reference. This might be a co-worker or acquaintance who has filed for

24

personal bankruptcy, or your religious leader, a social worker, or any person whose judgment you trust. Some trustees concentrate on personal bankruptcies and advertise their services on television, in newspapers or in your local telephone directory.

You should be seeking a trustee with whom you feel comfortable; someone who shows an understanding of your situation. Although the actual mechanical process will be conducted in the same way by anyone you choose, it always helps to work with someone who makes you feel comfortable as you go through the bankruptcy process – a personally stressful time.

2. Preparing To Meet With Your Trustee

Before meeting with the trustee, you should prepare a list of all your creditors and the approximate amount owing to each, a list of your assets and their approximate value, as well as a budget showing your total family monthly take-home income and your monthly living expenses. The trustee will need this information to conduct the initial assessment and to help you make a decision about whether or not bankruptcy is an appropriate course for you to take.

To assist you in gathering this information, many trustees will give you a form that helps you organize all of the relevant information. You could then complete this at home and bring it to your first meeting with the trustee. This will assist the trustee in understanding your situation and providing you with the appropriate alternatives. You will see from the example in Case Study 1 (p. 94) that a number of other questions are also asked, in order to anticipate any unusual issues which require attention from the trustee. Most importantly, they will also help you understand the effects of bankruptcy on your own personal situation before deciding whether or not to file for bankruptcy protection. We will review them in detail in Chapter 8.

3. The Initial Meeting

Your first meeting with the trustee is called an initial assessment. Under the Bankruptcy and Insolvency Act, a trustee must conduct an initial assessment of an insolvent person's affairs prior to accepting a file for bankruptcy. At this session, the trustee will review your financial situation and advise you of any alternatives to bankruptcy. These other options could be a proposal to your creditors, either informal, as discussed in Chapter 2, or formal (i.e., filed under the BIA), or, in certain provinces, entering into a debt repayment program. It is important to recognize that, if possible, you have an obligation to file a proposal to creditors rather than a bankruptcy. If a proposal is a viable alternative yet you choose bankruptcy, your creditors or your trustee could object to your automatic discharge (see p. 54). Most trustees do not charge a fee for this initial meeting.

6

    ——

Secured
Creditors

Before considering how bankruptcy affects your right to keep your assets, it is important to understand the rights of your secured creditors.

When you borrow money from anyone, that lender will always be concerned with your ability to repay the debt. In most cases, the creditor will accept your personal commitment to pay back the loan. This occurs, for example, with all credit cards. Your signature witnesses your intention to repay the credit granted and as long as you fulfil your side of the credit agreement, and pay at least the minimum monthly amount as agreed, the credit card grantor will continue to lend to you. If you do not pay as agreed, the creditor will have the right to sue for the amount owing and obtain judgment and execution against available assets which can be seized. These rights are the same for any *unsecured* debt which you incur, including even a loan guaranteed by a handshake.

But sometimes the creditor may be selling you an expensive asset which you cannot pay for in full on delivery, such as furniture, a car or even a house. In order to protect itself in the event that you do not pay when promised, the creditor will ask for a pledge of the purchased asset as *collateral* or *security* against nonpayment. For example, this could be a conditional sales contract with a finance company when buying furniture, or a mortgage given to a bank or trust company, when buying a house.

When you give your creditor a charge over an asset, that creditor becomes a *secured creditor* whose rights are now spelled out in a separate document or contract. As long as you pay the amounts agreed to in the contract, you retain the right to keep and enjoy the furniture, car or house which you pledged as security. If you miss payments or *default* on your obligations, your agreement will give the secured creditor certain rights to repossession and sale. You will be responsible for any shortfall if the proceeds of the sale cannot pay the whole debt in full.

The Bankruptcy and Insolvency Act does not interfere with secured creditors' rights, as granted by you in your contract with them. As long as the documentation has been properly registered in the appropriate registry sections of the provincial government, that creditor, in a bankruptcy, will be allowed to exercise its rights of seizure and sale under its security documents. However, this could only happen if you defaulted in your payments under the agreement.

This becomes very important when considering bankruptcy and its effect on your right to retain your assets.

7

What Happens to
My Assets?

When you file an assignment in bankruptcy, you must prepare a list of all of your assets and sign a sworn statement that you have made full disclosure. In all jurisdictions in Canada, there are provincial laws (such as the Ontario Executions Act) that protect certain assets from seizure, whether by your creditors or even by a trustee (on behalf of your creditors).

The following list considers some of the more common assets which you might own and a trustee's approach to dealing with them. The table of exemptions at the end of this chapter lists some of the major exemptions in different provinces. You should consult with a local trustee or lawyer to understand which exemptions apply to you.

ASSETS AND TREATMENT BY THE TRUSTEE

1. Personal Possessions

Personal possessions are protected from seizure by provincial legislation. For example, in Ontario, the Executions Act does not allow anyone to seize one's clothing and other personal possessions which have a value of less than $1,000. In practice, unless you have very valuable assets such as a collection of rare stamps or coins, valuable jewellery or art, your trustee and your creditors will usually not disturb your personal possessions. In my 20 years' of practice as a trustee, I have never been asked by creditors to visit anyone's home to inspect their personal possessions. In reality, our personal possessions seldom, if ever, have a significant resale value.

2. Furniture

The Ontario Executions Act protects your household furniture from seizure to the extent of $2,000 value per person. In practice, furniture seldom retains any significant value once it leaves the store. Consequently, this exemption is generally accepted by creditors in personal bankruptcies unless your furniture includes valuable pieces such as antiques that could be sold for the benefit of the bankruptcy estate.

Let us consider a situation where you have pledged your furniture as security to a finance company. Usually that used furniture will be worth far less than the secured debt. In bankruptcy, you have the option of returning it to the creditor. After selling the furniture, the secured creditor would file a claim with the trustee for any short-fall and would be treated in the same way as all the other unsecured creditors. In practice, finance companies are often willing to allow an individual to keep the furniture in return for negotiating a new loan in an amount that is closer to the true resale value of the furniture. This is allowable even though a bankruptcy has been filed, but you should review the arrangement with your trustee before signing.

3. Motor Vehicle

If your car is debt-free, it is an asset which the trustee must sell. The proceeds of sale belong to the bankruptcy estate, for the benefit of your creditors. However, in Ontario, every individual is allowed to retain *tools of a trade* (i.e., something needed in order to earn a living) up to a resale value of $2,000. If you must drive your car to earn a living (e.g., travelling salesperson), you may claim this exemption toward retaining the car. Often, if the value of the car is greater than $2,000, and you require the vehicle to perform your job, the trustee will allow you to have a friend or relative pay the excess value over the exemption to the trustee in order to retain the vehicle.

When a car is pledged as security for a loan from a bank or finance company, and its value is less than the amount owing on the loan, the car will have no net value (equity) to interest the trustee. In those instances, assuming your loan payments are all currently paid, you will probably have no problem keeping the car. On the other hand, if the car is worth more than the secured debt, and you can justify making the payments on the loan, you can usually keep the vehicle by having a third party (a friend or relative) pay the trustee the equity (the market value less the amount of the loan).

A trustee will also consider whether you really need a car, with its operating costs, after filing for bankruptcy, and could require that the car be returned to the secured creditor. All of these issues would be fully discussed with you by your trustee before filing the bankruptcy.

4. Home

Often by the time a person meets with a trustee, most, if not all, of the equity in the home has been either mortgaged or lost through collapsed market value. The trustee is only interested in the equity in the home. Equity is the amount of money that would be left to you if the home were sold, after paying the mortgage, taxes owing, sales commissions and legal expenses. If there is equity, rather than selling the home and realizing funds for the bankrupt estate, the trustee will usually be prepared to sell the estate's interest in the home to a third party (a friend or relative) for a fair price.

The mortgagee of your home is a secured creditor and has a separate contract with you, the mortgage. As long as you make your mortgage payments when due, the mortgagee must allow you to continue to own and occupy your home. Bankruptcy does not affect your mortgage, as long as the payments are current, and there is no equity in the home.

5. RRSP

Generally, any asset over which you exercise control becomes an asset of your bankruptcy estate. Many RRSP plans are payable to one's estate (upon death). In those cases the plans become controlled by the trustee in bankruptcy and will be collapsed and realized as an asset of the bankruptcy. However, certain plans which carry an irrevocable designation of another person as beneficiary, or which exist as part of an insurance policy, may be protected from seizure by a trustee. The rules regarding these situations are complex and depend upon the specific circumstances of each case. When you meet with a trustee, you will be advised of the trustee's position regarding this asset.

6. Life Insurance

There are many different types of life insurance products, but the majority fall into one of two categories – term or whole life.

Term insurance only has value when the insured dies and the benefit (face value) of the policy is paid to the beneficiary. Your filing for bankruptcy will not create any value in this type of policy and the trustee will have no interest in it. As long as you continue to pay the premiums, you can continue to maintain this insurance policy.

If your insurance is a whole life policy, it will contain a savings element and the longer you have been paying into it, the greater will be the accumulated value of savings. This value, or cash surrender value, can be borrowed from the insurer at any time. If your policy is payable to your estate and does not have a designated irrevocable beneficiary, a trustee has the same right to withdraw the current cash surrender value as you do. You may keep the insurance policy in force by continuing to pay the premiums, but a loan would then exist for which you will incur ongoing interest charges.

Provincial Exemptions from Seizure

Figure 1

PROVINCE	CLOTHING AND PERSONAL EFFECTS	HOUSEHOLD FURNITURE	TOOLS OF TRADE	AUTOMOBILE	HOME
British Columbia	necessary to debtor and family	$2,000	no specific provision	no specific provision	$2,500
Alberta	necessary to debtor and family	$4,000	$10,000	$5,000	$40,000
Saskatchewan	necessary to debtor and family	$4,500	$4,500	One car used for business	$32,000
Manitoba	necessary to debtor and family	$4,500	$7,500	$3,000	no provision
Ontario	$1,000	$2,000	$2,000	no specific provision	no provision
Quebec	$6,000 combined with furniture, auto	$6,000 combined with furniture, auto	$7,500	$6,000 combined with furniture, auto	$10,000
New Brunswick	necessary to debtor and family	$5,000	$200	$6,500 used for livelihood	no provision
Nova Scotia	necessary to debtor and family	necessary to debtor and family	$1,000	$3,000	no provision
Prince Edward Island	necessary to debtor and family	$2,000	$2,000	$3,000	no provision
Newfoundland	necessary to debtor and family	$5,000	$10,000	$5,000 used for livelihood	no provision

NOTE: *This chart highlights only some of the major exemptions from seizure provided by proincial statutes. To fully understand exactly which property is protected, you must obtain proper advice from your lawyer or trustee.*

8

———

Twelve Questions You'll Be Asked by Your Trustee

Let's assume that you have decided to file an assignment in bankruptcy. These are the questions which are asked as part of the initial assessment.

1. Have you been bankrupt before?

An individual bankrupt is automatically discharged from bankruptcy at the end of nine months from the date of filing. A certificate of discharge is then issued by the trustee, confirming that you have fulfilled all of your obligations as a bankrupt. At that time, officially, you have no further obligations to your trustee or to any of your bankruptcy creditors.

This provision does not apply in cases where a creditor, the trustee or the superintendent opposes the automatic discharge. As well, if a person has been bankrupt before, the discharge is not automatic. In all these instances, the discharge will be heard by a judge in bankruptcy court. If you were previously bankrupt, you should expect the court to extend the period until your discharge by at least a few months. As well, the court can impose other conditions as part of the your discharge from bankruptcy.

2. Have you applied for assistance through credit counselling, an orderly payment of debt program or voluntary deposit?

The trustee will want to know whether you have attempted to control your debt payments previously but failed. This must be taken into account when considering the realistic chances of successfully completing a proposal to your creditors under the BIA. After all, if you were unable to make the payments previously pledged under one of these programs, it may not be realistic to try again and bankruptcy may be the only meaningful option.

3. Are you bonded in your present position?

If you are bonded under a fidelity bond by your employer, this should not be affected unless the bankruptcy involves fraud or embezzlement. If the bond has been issued to you in business, you may have difficulty in obtaining this coverage after bankruptcy.

4. Have you received or do you expect to receive an inheritance?

You must appreciate that, as a condition of filing bankruptcy, you must give to the trustee the assets (subject to certain exemptions) which you own on the date of filing for bankruptcy. If you had an inheritance put aside for safekeeping, for example, this would belong to your creditors. As well, if you are expecting an inheritance in the foreseeable future, your trustee is required to collect this as an *after-acquired asset* and include it in the bankruptcy. The purpose of this is to prevent an individual from filing bankruptcy just before receiving a large inheritance, thus hoping to protect it from creditors.

5. Are there any writs, judgments, garnishments or wage assignments outstanding against you?

The filing of bankruptcy automatically stops all proceedings against you by your unsecured creditors. This is called a *stay of proceedings* and applies to all actions against you. It takes effect at the moment the bankruptcy is filed with the superintendent's office. If applicable, your trustee will notify the sheriff's office and your employer's payroll department to ensure that no more monies are taken from you by these creditors.

6. Have you been self-employed in the last five years?

This information is important for a number of reasons. Certain liabilities arise from running your own business, such as liability for employee tax deductions and GST remittances. As well, you will want to ensure that all of your creditors are notified of your bankruptcy. Under certain circumstances, a missed creditor can sometimes claim a payment from you even after you are discharged from bankruptcy.

7. Within the last 12 months have you:

(a) disposed of or transferred any of your assets?

Remember that the bankruptcy process is structured to be fair to both debtors and creditors. If you sell an asset for its fair value and can show that you have received full payment, usually there would be nothing wrong with the sale. However, if you sold a valuable asset to a friend or relative for a price well below fair value, or perhaps for just one dollar, and this took place within a short time before filing for bankruptcy, a creditor would be justified in assuming that the sale was just an attempt to protect your asset from seizure by the trustee on behalf of your creditors. For that reason, the BIA and other provincial legislation (such as the Ontario Assignments and Preferences Act and The Fraudulent

Conveyances Act) contain rules that will allow your trustee and creditors to review, challenge and possibly reverse these types of transfers, if improperly done.

(b) made payments in excess of regular payments to a creditor?

In order that all the creditors be treated fairly in a bankruptcy, the BIA allows the trustee to recover, in certain circumstances, payments made to creditors prior to bankruptcy. For example, if two months before filing for bankruptcy you used all your available cash to pay back a loan from a friend, and you had stopped paying any other creditors, a trustee would have the right to recover that payment from your friend. Those moneys would then become available for distribution to all your creditors, including your friend. If a payment were made to an immediate relative within 12 months prior to the bankruptcy, that too, could be attacked and recovered by the trustee.

(c) had any assets seized by any creditor?

Just as you may not show a preference by paying one creditor while not paying any others, so one creditor is not allowed to unlawfully seize assets from you in order to gain an advantage over the other creditors. Remember that assets can lawfully be seized by a secured creditor, or by a sheriff acting for a creditor who has obtained a judgment against you. Your trustee will want to review the seizure, and its circumstances and related documentation, to ensure that it was done correctly and was within the creditor's rights. Otherwise, the trustee may challenge the seizure and recover the assets or their value for the benefit of all the unsecured creditors.

8. Within the last five years have you:

(a) sold, disposed of or transferred any real estate?

(b) made any gifts to relatives or others in excess of $500?

These two questions also deal with your transferring of assets and relate to the effect the transfer had on your ability to pay your creditors. If the real estate was sold for fair value and you received the funds from the sale, then normally that transaction would not be challenged. But, for example, if you transferred the asset to your spouse and did not receive payment for the transfer, or if you gave large gifts to your children, and as a result could not pay your debts when due, those transfers and gifts might be challenged by the trustee.

9. Have you made arrangements to continue to pay any creditors?

The answer to this must be NO. Filing bankruptcy creates

a level playing field for all unsecured creditors. No payments may be made to these creditors after bankruptcy. The trustee now represents them and you must deal only with the trustee as the representative of all your unsecured creditors.

Often, secured creditors will allow the bankrupt to keep a secured asset and to continue to make payments. Subject to the trustee's review and agreement, these payments may be made after filing bankruptcy. For example, furniture pledged as security to a finance company is often kept after filing bankruptcy. The bankrupt may enter into a new contract with the finance company for an amount equal to the real value of the furniture, agreeing to make a series of payments, after which the debt will be fully paid. This type of transaction would usually be acceptable to a trustee.

10. Do you have a safety deposit box?

This question is asked to refresh your memory in case there are any assets or papers which should be delivered to the trustee.

11. Do you have any credit cards?

You are required to surrender all of your credit cards to the trustee, who will then return them to the card issuers. This includes cards which have low or even no balances outstanding. However, if your spouse is not filing bankruptcy and has a personal credit card on which you are a supplementary cardholder, you need not surrender that card since it remains as your spouse's liability, unaffected by your bankruptcy.

12. Does your spouse have any assets?

It is important to clarify which assets belong to which spouse and whether or not any previous transfer between spouses might be challenged. Your trustee will be looking for potential problems at this time and full disclosure must be made so that you can be properly advised before filing bankruptcy.

9

───

The Steps of
Bankruptcy

The bankruptcy process itself is relatively simple and straightforward for most people. There are 11 steps in the personal bankruptcy process.

1. Initial Assessment

When you first meet, your trustee will review your circumstances with you and provide you with answers to your concerns. This first meeting, or initial assessment, allows the trustee to understand your financial situation in order to advise you of your rights and obligations. As well, the trustee can then help you understand any alternatives to bankruptcy which might be available to you. Ultimately, you will make the decision as to whether or not bankruptcy is the appropriate solution to your problems.

Let us assume that you have decided to proceed with bankruptcy. Before filing the bankruptcy documents, you and your trustee will sign an assessment certificate, which confirms that you have had this assessment done prior to deciding to file an assignment in bankruptcy.

If you wish to see examples of the assessment certificate and the other related bankruptcy documents, refer to Case Study 1 on page 94.

2. The Documents

(a) The Assignment

To file bankruptcy, you must sign two main documents. The first of these is called an assignment. In it, you assign or give to the trustee (on behalf of your creditors) all of your possessions (assets). The trustee must sell these assets and collect the proceeds for future distribution to your creditors.

However, remember that not all assets are subject to seizure by the trustee. In the section regarding your assets, I have explained that every province has legislation which protects, within certain limits, your basic possessions such as clothing, furniture, car and personal items. You should refer back to that section and the chart on page 37 to more fully understand this protection.

(b) *Statement of Affairs*

If the only assets you have are exempt from seizure, or have equity of less than $5,000, your bankruptcy will be filed as a summary administration. If you have assets with an equity greater than $5,000, your bankruptcy will be filed as an ordinary administration. The statement of affairs you sign will differ according to the type of administration that applies to your circumstances, and the trustee's fees will be determined differently. Regardless of the form used, the steps of the bankruptcy process that follow will be basically the same.

The statement of affairs is really a net worth statement showing your assets and liabilities (i.e., debts). You must list all your assets, whether or not protected from seizure, as well as all your creditors, even if they are friends and relatives. List all possible debts, even those which are only guarantees. Remember that bankruptcy treats all your unsecured creditors equally.

The statement of affairs also includes a page of basic personal information, as well as your answers to some of the questions asked in the initial questionnaire you completed before filing.

3. The Actual Filing

After you have signed the required documents, your trustee will file the assignment and statement of affairs with the local office of the superintendent of bankruptcy. At that time you will be bankrupt.

4. Notice To Creditors

Within five days of your filing bankruptcy, your trustee will mail a notice to your creditors, informing them of the bankruptcy. Only creditors who hold at least 25 percent of the dollar value of the total claims filed with you and your trustee are in a position to request a meeting of creditors and they must do so within 30 days of your bankruptcy filing. If the request is made, the trustee will send out a formal notice inviting your creditors to a meeting.Creditors must file a proof of claim with the trustee if they wish to share in any distribution of bankruptcy monies to creditors. That is a document which states the amount owed to them. It is accompanied by the papers that support the debt (e.g., invoices, statements, etc.). The trustee will review these claims, compare them to the list that you prepared in your statement of affairs and may review them with you before accepting them.

This notice also informs your creditors that, in the case of a first-time bankrupt, unless someone files a notice of objection, you will be automatically discharged from bankruptcy nine months from the date of your filing bankruptcy. In practice, objections to discharge are seldom filed.

5. Examination

In a personal bankruptcy, there may be certain aspects which might concern a creditor, prompting him or her to seek further information. For that reason, the superintendent of bankruptcy's office, through an official receiver, may require that you go to the government office to be questioned about your financial affairs. The questions and answers will be documented and you will be required to formally swear that the answers are true. This is called an examination.

This examination provides a record of the circumstances of your bankruptcy, along with some financial information. The examination record will be made available to any creditors who request it. If an examination is requested, your trustee should review the questions you could be asked, before you are examined. Remember that this examination is done to collect information and should not be seen as a personal attack against you.

6. Creditors' Meeting

If a meeting of your creditors has been called, you must attend. This meeting is not a cross-examination. It is an opportunity for your creditors to ask questions and get information about your situation. After all, they are now unable to collect their debt and have a right to understand the circumstances. Often the meeting is held at the trustee's office and lasts less than half an hour. Your trustee will chair the meeting and will not allow anyone to act improperly. Since details of your financial affairs have already been sent to your creditors along with the notice of the meeting, you will often find that creditors do not come to the meeting.

7. The Counselling Sessions

Once a bankruptcy has been filed, most proceedings are rather routine. Over the course of the bankruptcy, you must make the monthly payments to the trustee as agreed when you filed bankruptcy and you must provide the trustee with the information necessary to prepare your personal income tax returns. You must also assist the trustee if any assets are to be sold. In addition, you must attend two counselling sessions, or you will not receive your automatic discharge and you may have to appear in court before a judge.

Within two months of filing bankruptcy, you are required to attend the first counselling session at the trustee's office. This session can be very valuable. The trustee will provide you with information and advice in the areas of money management, spending and shopping habits, obtaining and using credit and will alert you to the warning signs of financial difficulties.

The second counselling session will be held within seven months of filing bankruptcy. At this point, the trustee will continue to help you develop better money management and budgetary skills, as well as assisting in identifying any other factors which contributed to your financial problems. With the exception of attendances at the first meeting of creditors and these two mandatory counselling sessions, you will usually find that your life after bankruptcy begins to run smoothly without any interaction with your creditors.

8. Discharge From Bankruptcy

(a) Automatic (Unopposed)

At last, nine months have passed. You attended the creditors' meeting, kept up your monthly payments to the trustee, assisted the trustee as required and attended the counselling sessions. In the meantime your trustee has notified the creditors of your discharge date. Usually a person's bankruptcy-related affairs are relatively straightforward and creditors do not object to the discharge. If no objections are received, the trustee will sign the certificate of discharge effective nine months from the day that you filed bankruptcy. You should receive a copy of that certificate for your personal records.

Upon receipt of the certificate of discharge, you are no longer bankrupt and usually have no further financial obligations to either your creditors or to the trustee representing them in the process. You can proceed with your life, building a better future for yourself and your family. However you should be aware of certain exceptions to the discharge of your debts. These are more fully covered on pages 63–66.

(b) Opposed

In some cases, a creditor may oppose your automatic discharge for any one of a number of reasons. The creditor may feel the payments you made voluntarily to the trustee during bankruptcy were insufficient, or that you had the ability and chose not to file a proposal for a greater return to your creditors, and that a judge should review the file to consider requiring additional payments as a condition of discharge. Or the creditor may feel your actions before filing bankruptcy were improper or misleading and that your discharge should be reviewed by a judge who might consider withholding discharge as punishment for those actions. Or the creditor might just be angry and vengeful and file the opposition as a matter of principle. Your trustee will explain these situations to you when you first meet and alert you to the possible problems which might result in a creditor opposing discharge.

Remember that oppositions to discharge are relatively few and almost always result from something you will likely be aware of when filing. When discharges are opposed, you are assured of a fair hearing before a judge who will take your statements into consideration. Again, your trustee will advise you as to the likelihood of an opposition to your discharge.

If a bankrupt has not performed his or her duties and responsibilities during bankruptcy, or has perhaps been uncooperative, the trustee would probably oppose the bankrupt's discharge. But, in the vast majority of cases, bankrupts do cooperate and assist the trustee and are discharged with no opposition filed.

9. Trustee's Completion Of Your File

Although you may already be discharged, your trustee must still complete the work on your file. In that regard, you will usually still have at least one further responsibility – to gather the information needed for the trustee to prepare your post-bankruptcy income tax return. This will happen when you get your year-end information slips, usually in February.

10. Payment of Dividends To Creditors

During your bankruptcy, the trustee maintained a separate trust bank account in your name. The monthly payments which you made to the trustee were deposited to that account. In addition, if the trustee collapsed an RRSP, sold a car or collected a tax refund, all of these and any other realizations went into that account.

When the administration of your bankruptcy is finalized, the trustee has its fees approved by the superintendent of bankruptcy and, in some situations, by the court.

The balance in the trust account, after payment of the trustee's fees, is then distributed pro rata to all the creditors who have filed a claim in the bankruptcy. This means that the money is shared by those creditors in proportion to the amount you owed them.

11. Trustee's Discharge

After all the money in the trust account is distributed to the eligible creditors, your trustee will prepare a final report and be discharged. Your file will be kept in storage for a number of years, in case it must be referred to. Otherwise, you and your trustee are finished with the administration of your bankruptcy.

Figure 2 **Steps in the Bankruptcy Process**	
TIMING	
Start	Initial assessment Filing of bankruptcy
Within 5 days of filing	Trustee mails notice of bankruptcy and notice of automatic nine-month discharge to all creditors
In first few weeks	Examination (if required)
Thirty days from filing	Trustee calls meeting of creditors (if requested) Meeting of creditors (if called)
Within two months of filing	First counselling session
Within seven months of filing	Second counselling session
In eighth month after filing	Trustee prepares report to superintendent of bankruptcy
Nine months after date of filing	If no one opposes discharge, trustee issues certificate of discharge

10

Other
Matters

1. Petitions – Another Path Into Bankruptcy

Any creditor owed a debt of more than $1,000 can petition the court to place the debtor in bankruptcy. If the court agrees, it will issue a receiving order. This is a court order that appoints a trustee to take custody of your assets in order to sell them for the benefit of your unsecured creditors.

This is a serious step for a creditor to take. Your creditor may not know what assets you own or who your other creditors are and if you are put into bankruptcy, the petitioning creditor will have to guarantee its lawyer's and trustee's costs which would probably be about $3,000 to $4,000, and could be significantly higher. These may not be recoverable from a bankruptcy.

In order to successfully petition you into bankruptcy, your creditor must prove in court that you have committed an act of bankruptcy, the one most commonly cited being "failure to pay debts when they are due."

Your creditor may have already successfully sued you, obtained judgment and asked the sheriff to attempt to seize your personal assets in order to satisfy the debt. If the sheriff confirms that you do not have available assets to settle the debt, that evidence is usually sufficient for the court to issue a receiving order to put you into bankruptcy.

If several of your creditors confirm in court that, during the previous six months, they have unsuccessfully attempted to collect their due debts, this could also be a satisfactory argument for a receiving order to be issued against you.

If a petition is filed against you, you have ten days in which to file a defence in court. That filing will bring the matter before a judge who will then hear the arguments from both you and your creditor and will decide whether or not a receiving order should be issued.

If you do not file a defence against the petition within ten days, a receiving order will be issued on the date of the hearing.

Sometimes, although you may be insolvent and have no argument to present, you may still be able to settle your debts within the framework of a proposal. If within the ten day period, you file a proposal or a notice of intent to file a proposal, this will act as a stay of proceedings and freeze the action under the petition. You will then be able to attempt to settle your debts within a proposal.

If the proposal is accepted by the required majority of your creditors, the petition will not proceed any further and you can continue under the terms agreed in the proposal. On the other hand, if the proposal is not accepted by your creditors, your bankruptcy will usually follow. A failed consumer proposal will allow the petition to proceed to court and a receiving order will likely be issued. A failed ordinary proposal will automatically result in bankruptcy. Proposals are fully discussed in the section starting on page 75.

2. Determining Monthly Payments To Your Trustee

When you file bankruptcy, you no longer have direct obligations to pay your unsecured creditors. This relief usually allows you enough money to cover your regular living expenses with perhaps some "excess" money left over. The Bankruptcy and Insolvency Act requires a bankrupt to make monthly payments to the trustee on behalf of the creditors. These payments continue while you are in bankruptcy, usually for nine months.

In order to calculate the monthly amount that you are required to pay to your trustee while in bankruptcy, your trustee will refer to a set of guidelines produced annually by the superintendent of bankruptcy. When your bankruptcy is filed, your trustee must report your commitment to payments during the nine months of bankruptcy to the superintendent in bankruptcy. That report must either confirm the amount required by the guidelines or must contain allowable adjustments for extraordinary expenses (such as alimony or child support). If you cannot agree with your trustee as to the monthly payment, the superintendent, upon filing of the bankruptcy, can attempt to mediate an acceptable payment. If this cannot be achieved, the determination can be referred to a judge.

The schedule on page 61 was developed from the Guidelines set by the superintendent of bankruptcy for 1998. When you meet with a trustee, the calculation will be reviewed and explained. Certain special expenses are also allowed which will reduce the required monthly payments.

From this table, for example, a bankrupt with two dependents and a monthly after-tax income of $2,570 would have to make monthly payments of $140 during the nine months of bankruptcy.

3. Credit Cards

When the Bankruptcy and Insolvency Act was amended in November 1992, provision was made requiring all persons

Figure 3   **Required Monthly Payments While in Bankruptcy Based on Superintendent's Standards**

1998

# of persons	NET MONTHLY FAMILY INCOME														
	1570	1670	1770	1970	2170	2370	2570	2770	2970	3170	3370	3570	3770	3970	4170
1	50	100	150	250	350	450	550	650	750	850	950	1050	1150	1250	1350
2				65	115	265	365	465	565	665	765	865	965	1065	1165
3							140	240	340	440	540	640	740	840	940
4									100	200	300	400	500	600	700
5											140	240	340	440	540
6												75	175	275	375
7														220	420

filing bankruptcy to surrender all existing credit cards. This applies even if the card is fully paid and carries no balance. Your trustee is required to collect all the credit cards from you at the time of filing bankruptcy.

4. Income Tax Returns

Your trustee is required to prepare and file your personal income tax returns for the previous year (if outstanding) and the tax returns for the year in which you are filing bankruptcy. The year of bankruptcy is divided into two tax years. The trustee will prepare and file an income tax return for the period from January 1 until the actual date of bankruptcy. This is called the pre-bankruptcy tax return. You must provide the trustee with the information necessary to file this return. If any tax is owing on this return, it is included along with your other creditors in the bankruptcy.

As well, you will be asked to assign any refund that results from the filing of the post-bankruptcy tax return which covers the period from the date of bankruptcy until the end of the calendar year. When you receive the usual information slips (such as a T4 from your employer, a T5 for interest earned, etc.) your trustee will calculate the income for the post-bankruptcy period and file the return.

If you are expecting a tax refund at the time of filing

bankruptcy, that refund will represent an asset which the trustee will take on behalf of your creditors.

Also, GST cheques payable to you for approximately one and a half years from the bankruptcy date will be directed by Revenue Canada to the trustee.

5. Debts Not Discharged By Bankruptcy

As a general rule, all personal debts are released by bankruptcy. This includes such debts as credit cards, personal loans, and debts to governments such as personal income taxes and directors' liability for corporate tax and other government remittances.

(a) Secured Debt

One important exception to this rule is secured debt. The liability on an existing house mortgage or a car loan, for example, continues through and after bankruptcy, but is limited to the value of the secured assets. If those assets are returned to the secured creditor, or disposed of, your liability for any shortfall is an unsecured debt which is discharged in a bankruptcy.

(b) Student Loans

Until September 1997, student loans owing to both federal and provincial governments were treated the same as any other unsecured debts. Then the law was changed to prohibit a debtor from including any student loans in a bankruptcy if the debtor had not completed studies at least two years before filing for bankruptcy. No sooner was the law passed and implemented than the rules changed again. Effective June 19, 1998, student loans incurred within ten years of filing cannot be included in the bankruptcy.

Once the ten-year period has expired, a debtor can go to court and, based upon the individual's income and circumstances at that time, ask that the debt be settled or extinguished. Although not enough time has passed to assess the impact of these changes, it appears that the government will be free to pursue collection from the time of the person's discharge from bankruptcy until the matter can be settled through the courts.

(c) Liability of a Guarantor

In some situations, although *your* liability for a debt will be released by your personal bankruptcy, a guarantor, such as your spouse, who might have co-signed for your loan, will still be responsible for payment. It is important to examine all your debts and to understand how bankruptcy will affect a guarantor.

(d) *Fraudulently Obtained Debts*

Since bankruptcy is intended to help honest debtors who have no other way to solve their financial problems, it is understandable that debts obtained through fraud are not released by bankruptcy. If an individual has been found guilty of criminal fraud, any debts created by that fraud will not be forgiven in a bankruptcy and will still be owing by that person.

Fraud can exist where false information has been given in order to obtain a loan. Suppose, for example, that when applying for a loan you provided a personal net worth statement that overstated your assets or did not disclose all of your debts. That creditor may object to your discharge from bankruptcy and may be able to prove that the loan was obtained through your provision of false information. If the fraud can be established, that debt will not be extinguished by bankruptcy and will still have to be paid afterwards.

(e) *Court Ordered Debts*

Also, any debts imposed by a court order, including penalties and fines such as parking tickets, will not be discharged and will still have to be paid after bankruptcy. Although arrears of alimony and child support payments rank as a preferred claim in the bankruptcy, ahead of other ordinary unsecured creditors, the liability for any unpaid balance of arrears and the ongoing payments of alimony and support will continue after bankruptcy.

(f) Forgotten Creditors

And finally, if you neglected to list a creditor when you filed bankruptcy, and if that creditor learns of your bankruptcy after you have been discharged, you will still be liable, but only for the payment the creditor would have received from the trustee had that creditor been included.

6. Wage Garnishments

(a) Judgment Creditor

If you have been sued by an unsecured creditor and the court has issued a judgment against you for that debt, your creditor has the right to ask the sheriff's office (provincial attorney-general's department) to collect the debt from you. This is called execution after judgment.

The sheriff can, for example, then seize money from your bank account or issue your employer a demand for direct payment of a portion of your wages. This is called a wage garnishment and once issued continues until the debt is fully paid. Often this results in deductions of as much as 20 percent of your wages. The sheriff is required to hold these monies for 30 days before paying them to your judgment creditors.

How is this affected by bankruptcy? If you file an assignment in bankruptcy,

(i) The filing immediately stops the garnishment. Your trustee will notify the sheriff's office and your employer that you are bankrupt and that the garnishment is stayed or stopped.

(ii) The trustee will demand and receive any money collected by the sheriff in the last 30 days – money being held before payment to your judgment creditors. This money then becomes an asset in your bankruptcy and will be kept by the trustee for eventual distribution to all of your creditors.

After filing for bankruptcy protection, you will receive your full wages.

(b) Wage Assignment To A Credit Union

Often, loans given by a credit union are supported by an assignment of wages as security.

If you do not make your committed payments to the credit union, the assignment of wages can be presented to your employer. This particular assignment usually follows you from job to job. Your employer will be required to deduct the amount assigned, usually 20 percent of your wages, and remit it to the credit union.

Bankruptcy stops the operation of the wage

assignment. Your trustee will immediately notify the credit union and your employer when you file bankruptcy or a proposal and no more deductions can be taken from your wages.

7. The Trustee's Fees

Who Pays The Trustee?

When you file bankruptcy or a proposal, your trustee will maintain a separate estate bank account for your file. All the money collected by the trustee in connection with your file will be kept in this account. In a bankruptcy, for example, this could include your monthly payments, income tax refunds, proceeds from the sale of a car and money obtained by collapsing an RRSP. In a proposal money would usually come from you as monthly payments for an agreed period of time.

In either a bankruptcy or a proposal, the Bankruptcy and Insolvency Act lists the order in which the estate funds are to be distributed. The trustee's fees are usually the first payment made. Therefore, the trustee is paid out of the estate and not directly by you.

This is important to understand because when a trustee agrees to handle your file, the trustee will want to ensure that your estate will accumulate sufficient money to pay the trustee's fees. For example, if you are unemployed, have no assets, and therefore cannot even make minimum monthly payments in your bank-ruptcy, you will probably be asked by the trustee to have a friend or relative guarantee that the estate will have enough money to pay the trustee's minimum fee.

How Much Does A Trustee Charge?

The amount that a trustee charges an estate is set out in the Bankruptcy and Insolvency Act. In the case of small estates, such as a summary administration bankruptcy or a consumer proposal, the minimum prescribed fees are as follows:

(a) **Summary Bankruptcy** (assets less than $5,000) **Fee Allowed**

Basic fee	$ 975
Two Counselling Sessions	170
	1,145
Add: GST	80
Administrative disbursements	100
Filing fee	50
Total Minimum Fee	$1,375

If the total funds in the estate are greater than $1,375, the trustee's fee increases by prescribed percentages of the additional funds.

Since there are no government programs in place to pay the trustee's fees, such as there are for Legal Aid, a trustee will usually want to be satisfied that at least $1,375 will come into the estate bank account so that the minimum prescribed fee or tariff will be covered.

(b) **Consumer Proposal**   **Fee Allowed**

Basic fee	$1,500
Two Counselling Sessions	170
	$1,670
Add: GST	117
Filing fee	50
	$1,837

Plus 20% of all monies distributed to the creditors

In practice the first $1,837 paid by you into a consumer proposal goes toward the trustee's fees. Thereafter, the trustee will deduct twenty percent of each payment made to your creditors. For example, using this calculation, if your payments under a consumer proposal are $250 per month for three years, you will have paid a total of $9,000. Of this, the trustee will be paid $1,837 plus twenty percent of the distribution to creditors of $7,163 or $1,432, for a total fee of $3,269. The balance of $5,631 will be the net distribution to your creditors under the proposal.

In the case of an ordinary administration bankruptcy or an ordinary proposal, the trustee must have its fees approved by the provincial supreme court and also by the inspectors, who are representatives of your creditors. Inspectors are elected at the first meeting of creditors. Fees in these files reflect the professional time spent in the administration and management of more complex issues.

In this ordinary administration bankruptcy or proposal, as in the less complex files, a trustee will want to be satisfied, before accepting a file, that a reasonable estimate of the expected fees will be guaranteed to be paid. Often, the minimum fees are guaranteed by a friend or relative.

Very few situations arise in which a trustee is unable to work out a suitable arrangement regarding fees. This will always be reviewed in your initial meeting with the trustee, so you need not worry about it. As well, many trustees across Canada participate in a voluntary program with the superintendent of bankruptcy, to ensure that any person who genuinely needs to file bankruptcy will be able to do so, despite having insufficient funds to cover the total cost of the bankruptcy. In fact, very few situations require this special facility.

8. Credit Bureaus And Credit Ratings

In order to understand the effect of bankruptcy on your credit, you must understand what a credit bureau is, how your credit rating is determined and what factors can change that rating.

You should get to know the credit bureau in your area because it already knows a lot about you. The credit bureau probably has a record of your financial dealings – a late payment on your credit card, a bounced cheque, an application for credit, etc. Equifax Canada Inc. accounts for approximately 90 percent of the consumer credit information market. It collects credit information to sell to financial institutions so they can rate your credit worthiness or risk. Financial institutions ultimately decide on a person's credit worthiness, but usually base their decisions on the information contained in the Equifax files. The information contained in the Equifax files can determine whether or not your application for a credit card, loan or mortgage will be approved. The files retain all credit information – both good and bad – for a period of seven years. Therefore, it is important that you check your file at Equifax, especially if you are planning to apply for a loan from a financial institution.

You can easily obtain a print-out from your file at Equifax by telephone. You will be asked to provide your name, date of birth, social insurance number, present and last address, and a credit card number and within seven business days Equifax will send a print-out to you. If there is any inaccurate information, you should provide proof to Equifax so they can update your file with the necessary changes.

The following are the different credit ratings which may be recorded in your file as information is regularly reported by your creditors:

R0   Too new to rate.

R1   Pays within 30 days, and all payments are up

to date.

R2   Pays in 30 to 60 days, and is not more than one payment behind.

R3   Pays in 60 to 90 days, or is two payments behind.

R4   Pays in 90 to 120 days, or is three or more payments behind.

R5   Account is at least 120 days overdue, but not in collection.

R7   Making regular payments under consolidation order or similar arrangements (e.g., proposals)

R8   In repossession.

R9   Account is in collection or debtor cannot be found (e.g., in bankruptcy).

You should know what information is reflected on your credit record at all times. Call your local Equifax office now to request your ratings.

Remember that almost all of your unsecured creditors report monthly to Equifax. Therefore, your credit record shows not only late payments but also the payments you make on time. The trick is to build up a record of good payment history – R1 ratings. For further information about the steps to be taken, see Chapter 12, Life After Debt – A New Beginning.

11

——

Proposals to Creditors: The Consumer Proposal and the Ordinary Proposal

WHICH CREDITORS ARE DEALT WITH IN A PROPOSAL?
When presenting a proposal, you can decide which classes of creditors will be included. You may address the proposal to only the unsecured creditors, or you can also include secured creditors. Usually secured creditors are dealt with separately and are not included as participants in a proposal.

For example, if you are one month behind in payments to a bank on a secured car loan, you will likely arrange with the bank to catch up on the payment after the proposal to unsecured creditors is approved and in place. In this case, your proposal would not necessarily include any provision for the secured creditor and the bank might not be formally involved at all.

Depending upon your personal situation, your trustee will assist you in determining which groups of creditors should be included in the proposal.

ORDER OF DISTRIBUTION OF FUNDS

The Bankruptcy and Insolvency Act sets out the order in which funds are to be distributed in a bankruptcy or in a proposal. The money in an estate must be paid out as follows:

(1) If the debtor was self-employed and had employees with income taxes withheld at source, the first funds will be used to pay any arrears of remittances to Revenue Canada for these amounts.

(2) The trustee's administration costs. This includes the trustee's fees and any legal or other expenses incurred by the trustee.

(3) Claim for up to one year's arrears of alimony or child support.

(4) Usually the balance of funds in a personal bankruptcy or proposal will be distributed among the remaining unsecured creditors. (Remember that this group includes, among others, credit card balances, personal loans, bank debts, and even government claims such as personal income tax, GST and sales tax.)

The Bankruptcy and Insolvency Act provides two paths for an individual who wishes to present a proposal to his or her creditors – a consumer proposal or an ordinary proposal.

CONSUMER PROPOSAL

This approach may be used by any person whose total debts (excluding the home mortgage) are less than $75,000. This type of proposal is usually filed by individuals who are wage earners – people who are on fixed and regular incomes. There is a very important limitation to this process. A consumer proposal can only be made once, and therefore, it is critical that your offer to creditors be the best possible. If refused, the only other alternative available to you may be bankruptcy.

These are the main steps in a consumer proposal:

1. A consumer proposal is filed through an administrator, an individual authorized by the superintendent of bankruptcy to accept and manage consumer proposals. All trustees in bankruptcy are administrators; in certain provinces other individuals are also permitted to act as administrators of a consumer proposal.

2. You begin the process by meeting with an administrator for an initial assessment. At that time, the administrator will review your personal finances and

determine whether or not it is possible to present a meaningful offer to your creditors.

3. You will then prepare your proposal, which is usually an offer to pay a percentage of your debt, by paying to the administrator a fixed amount each month for a certain period, normally two or three years.

4. Your administrator then files this proposal with the superintendent of bankruptcy, at which time all actions against you will be stayed or frozen, just as they are in a bankruptcy.

5. The administrator then mails the proposal, including your personal net worth statement, to your creditors and requests that they consider the offer.

6. In the case of a consumer proposal, three different outcomes are possible:

   (i)   No creditor objects to the proposal within 45 days. The proposal is then considered to have been approved by your creditors and, after an additional period of 15 days to allow for any appeal of the deemed acceptance of your proposal, you will begin to make the agreed payments to the administrator on behalf of your creditors.

   (ii) A creditor objects, or more than 25% of votes received by the trustee are against the proposal, prompting a meeting and a vote to be taken at that meeting. If the proposal is approved by a majority of the creditors who vote (based on dollars owed), you will then begin to make the payments to the administrator in accordance with the proposal.

(iii) If the consumer proposal is refused by your creditors, either by voting letters or at a meeting, the stay of proceedings against you is ended and you and your creditors are left in the same position as before the proposal was made and any collection actions could continue against you.

7. Assuming that the consumer proposal is approved, you will then begin to make the payments to your administrator as agreed. Within two months of the proposal date, you will meet with your administrator for a counselling session. This will be an opportunity for you to obtain information relating to money management and the wise use of credit.

8. As long as the monthly payments are made on time, the administrator and your creditors will not interfere with your banking, your job or anything else in your life.

9. A second counselling session will be held within seven months of the date of the proposal. At that

time, your administrator will continue to offer help in money management and will also give you an opportunity to consider, where applicable, other problems which may have caused your financial difficulties.

10. When you have completed your proposal and made all the payments, your administrator will provide you with a certificate of full performance, confirming that you have fulfilled all of your commitments under the proposal. At that time, you will have no further responsibility for the debts settled in your proposal. As well, your creditors will no longer have any right to collect the unpaid balance.

Figure 4 **Steps in a Consumer Proposal**	
TIMING	**STEPS IN THE CONSUMER PROPOSAL**
Start	Meet with administrator/trustee for initial assessment – develop proposal
	Proposal filed – mailed to creditors
45 days after filing	If no objection – approved (see performance below)
	If objection, hold creditors' meeting
	Defeated – no further activity Approved – see performance below
Within two months of filing	Performance – first counselling session
Monthly	Agreed payments to administrator
At times provided in proposal	Administrator distributes payments to creditors
Within seven months of filing	Second counselling session
Completion	Administrator issues certificate of full performance

ORDINARY PROPOSAL

The ordinary proposal was used originally by corporations wishing to reorganize their debts with their creditors, but over the years its application expanded to include individuals. Today, this type of proposal is used by any individual who does not qualify for the consumer proposal. Generally, these are people who are self-employed and who often have assets which they are attempting to retain. Doctors, lawyers, accountants, salespeople (e.g., brokers of insurance and real estate) and small unincorporated business owners are all examples of people who might file an ordinary proposal. Unlike the consumer proposal, rejection of an ordinary proposal results in immediate bankruptcy.

These are the main steps in an ordinary proposal:

1. Meet with your trustee for an initial review and assessment of your financial situation. If appropriate, a notice of intent to file a proposal can be filed. The trustee then files this notice with the superintendent of bankruptcy and mails it to your creditors. The notice of intent acts as a stay of all creditors' collection activities, freezing their position. This freeze continues for 30 days.

2. Within ten days of filing the notice, you must file with the trustee a statement of projected cash flow, showing your expected cash income and expenditures for the next several months. Your

trustee will file this with the superintendent of bankruptcy and will give a copy to any of your creditors who request one.

3. Before the expiry of the 30 day stay period, a proposal must be filed with your trustee. The trustee will assist you in its preparation. After filing, the trustee will send the proposal to all of your creditors with a report on your financial situation, explaining why the acceptance of the proposal is to your creditors' advantage. Creditors are also given notice of a meeting to be held within three weeks, to consider and to vote on the proposal.

   In presenting the proposal to your creditors, the trustee must be able to demonstrate that if the proposal is rejected and you are thereby placed into bankruptcy, they will recover less than the amount offered in your proposal.

   In practice the process is often started directly by filing a proposal. Usually the notice of intent and the extra 30 day stay are used in situations which require instant relief – when there is insufficient time available to prepare and file a full proposal.

4. At the creditors' meeting, your creditors will have an opportunity to ask you questions regarding your situation and your offer. You can even change and improve the proposal at that meeting. A vote on

the proposal is then taken. To have the proposal . approved and thus make it binding on all of your creditors, you must obtain support from more than half of the creditors who vote. As well, those creditors supporting the proposal must represent at least two-thirds of the total dollars owed to all creditors voting at that meeting.

Voting can be by mail or in person at the meeting. Creditors can be approached by you or your trustee prior to the meeting and voting letters obtained ahead of the meeting.

5. If the proposal is not approved, you will be deemed to be bankrupt and the trustee handling the proposal will automatically become trustee in your personal bankruptcy. The meeting of creditors on the proposal then becomes the meeting of creditors on your bankruptcy, and all procedures after that are the same as described earlier for personal bankruptcy.

6. On the other hand, let's be positive! If the proposal is approved by your creditors, the trustee will proceed to bring the proposal to court for approval. This approval is withheld only in rare circumstances.

7. After court approval, you will begin to fulfil your obligations as agreed in the proposal. These may involve transferring of certain moneys or other

assets to your trustee and/or making a series of payments to the trustee.

8. Once you have completed all obligations under the proposal, your trustee will issue you a certificate of full performance. At that time, you will have no further obligations to either the trustee or to your creditors under the proposal regarding the balance of debt remaining.

Figure 5 **Steps in the Ordinary Proposal**	
TIMING	STEPS IN THE ORDINARY PROPOSAL
Start	Meet trustee for initial assessment. If critical, file notice of intent to file a proposal
Within five days of filing notice of intent	Trustee notifies all creditors of 30 day stay of proceedings
Within ten days of filing notice of intent	File projected cash flow statement
Within 30 days of filing notice of intent	Prepare and file proposal.Trustee mails to creditors with notice of meeting to vote on proposal
Within three weeks of filing proposal	Creditors' meeting. If defeated, immediate bankruptcy (see steps of bankruptcy chart) If approved, continue with performance
Monthly	Performance – agreed payments to trustee
Every 90 days	Performance – trustee distributes payments to creditors
Completion	Trustee issues certificate of full performance and finalizes file

12

Life After Debt –
A New Beginning

Well, congratulations! You have filed for bankruptcy protection, worked with your trustee, made payments as
agreed, no one has objected to your discharge, and you
have just received your certificate of discharge (if you filed
bankruptcy) or your certificate of full performance (if you
made a proposal).

It is now time to begin building a new credit record.
Your income and expenses should now be under control,
budgeted and carefully managed. The following steps will
help you begin to establish a good credit rating:

1. Visit your local credit bureau. Provide them with
    a copy of your certificate of discharge or full per-
    formance, and ensure that it is noted on your cred-
    it record. Also, the credit bureau should delete all

the details of your previous financial dealings on your record. They will also allow you to put a short explanatory note on to your record.

2. Next, visit your banker. It is helpful to develop a relationship here. If your banker is aware of, and understands, your personal history and your changed circumstances, he or she can be of considerable assistance in helping you to establish a new credit record.

    A few steps towards developing that banking relationship are to:

    (a) Maintain all of your accounts at the same bank branch, and choose a bank that was not a creditor in your bankruptcy or proposal proceedings. You want a fresh start!

    (b) Set up a savings account as soon as possible and begin to put money aside on a regular basis. The amount is not as important as the fact that you are actually saving.

    (c) Start an RRSP, even if the amount is not large.

    (d) Ensure that you maintain your chequing account carefully, never allowing any cheques to be returned NSF.

    Taking these steps will show that you are a person who is acting responsibly in terms of financial planning. You will be, and will appear to be, a person to whom credit can be granted with little or no risk.

(e) Once you have accumulated a small amount of savings, say $500, borrow that amount from your bank. Explain that the purpose of this loan is to create a record of borrowing and repayment. Leave your savings account as security for the loan and do not remove the borrowed funds from the bank. Repay the loan from the borrowed funds over five months, supplementing it with enough to cover the interest on the loan.

You have now created a loan history that can be referred to by your banker, if asked for a reference.

Your relationship with the bank will bring benefits in new situations. If you are applying for credit from your banker, you will have a record which speaks well for you. If your credit application is to another credit grantor, you will have established a relationship and borrowing history that allows you to get a good credit reference from your banker.

3. Another approach to establishing a credit rating is through new credit cards. After discharge from

bankruptcy, or after completing your proposal, apply for a private label credit card – these are usually issued by retail chains. Often, these merchants recognize that you are likely a very good credit risk at this point in time, since you still have your income but have no debt.

Begin using the card immediately. Ensure that the amount charged is small enough that you can budget for payment when due. You should, at this stage, have the cash in your bank account, put aside to pay this bill.

When you receive your monthly statement, immediately pay the account in full. Continue to use this card every month and to pay it in full as soon as the statement arrives.

As a result of this process, the credit card issuer will be providing the credit bureau with a monthly record of your charges and your prompt full payments. After five or six months of such credit activity, apply for a second private card, continuing the same process now for both cards.

Assuming that you now have full control over your financial affairs, and once you have one or more years of good credit reports accumulating on your credit bureau file, you should begin to consider your ongoing credit needs.

4. You will likely want to obtain a general purpose bank credit card that will allow you to easily arrange hotels, accommodations, theatre tickets, rent an automobile, etc. Recognize that your bankruptcy will be carried on your credit record for seven years. However, the more time that passes since the filing of bankruptcy, the less important that history will be in obtaining new credit. More important will be your ongoing credit record since the bankruptcy.

   If you are applying for a bank credit card, you should discuss this first with the banker you have dealt with since the filing. If you have developed a good relationship, you may be surprised by the assistance available at your bank.

   As well, a letter of reference from your banker will be advantageous in any credit application.

Rebuilding your credit rating is a process which may take several years. Therefore, it is very important that you begin as soon as possible. These are only a few examples of steps which you can take. Remember that the purpose of establishing new credit facilities is not to obtain credit merely because it has again become available but to establish a good credit rating which is critical in such circumstances as purchasing a home or car. It is to this end that your rating must be improved and you must never allow yourself to be again caught in the debt spiral that you have worked out of.

Generally, the longer you demonstrate that you are responsibly handling your personal financial obligations, the greater the chances are that a new creditor will have the confidence to extend credit to you.

Conclusion

If there is just one message I can leave with you, it is that you can take control of your personal finances. If your circumstances are such that you require a bankruptcy or a proposal to regain control, you should see these steps for what they are – straightforward legal processes that bring you and your creditors together for a final settlement of your debts.

I have reviewed the most important commonly encountered issues. There are no secret agendas in the bankruptcy process. The law and rules were written to ensure that your rights and those of your creditors are protected and respected.

If you file for bankruptcy protection, your trustee will respect those rights. Now that you have more information on how the system works, I hope that you will be able to take control of your financial life. And if you cannot settle your affairs with your creditors, you can now make an informed decision about whether bankruptcy or a proposal offers the necessary solution.

I believe, very strongly, that a trustee's role is not only to protect the creditors' rights, but also to protect your rights and to help you face your difficulties and overcome them, to give a fresh start to your life.

CASE STUDIES

Names used in these case studies are entirely fictitious. Any similarity to actual persons is purely coincidental.

Case Study 1
HAROLD AND MARY JONES:
A PERSONAL BANKRUPTCY

In 1993, when Harold and Mary Jones moved from Montreal to Toronto, they were excited and anxious to begin their new life. Harold's employer, ABC Sales Inc., had a sales opening at the North York head office in the computer sales division. With his expertise in computer sales and an increase in salary, Harold saw the move as a great opportunity.

Living costs were, as they expected, higher than in Montreal, but the Joneses were able to buy a three-bedroom bungalow for $225,000, using the equity of $70,000 from their Montreal home for a down payment.

Mary had intended to continue working part time as a kindergarten teacher in Toronto to help compensate for the higher cost of living. Unfortunately, there were no positions available, and that second income never materialized. But, by being frugal and watching their expenses carefully, the Joneses were able to get by. Harold was hoping that, being a top salesman at head office, he would have an opportunity to advance quickly at ABC Sales Inc.

Reality struck hard in November 1996 when, after suffering significant operating losses, ABC Sales Inc. had to lay off Harold. After exhausting the severance pay and Employment Insurance benefits, and still unable to find another job, Harold began to fall behind in the monthly payments on his credit cards and bank loan.

In September 1997, ABC Sales Inc.'s operations had begun to improve, and Harold was rehired. But his debts were overwhelming. Telephone calls from creditors and collection agencies continued, and there was no end in sight.

When Harold and Mary came to see me in April 1998, they were at their wit's end. The mounting pressures of debt were enormous, and their tension and stress were visible.

They had completed the questionnaire and summary of monthly income and expenses, and we reviewed it together. (See pages 96–100.)

QUESTIONNAIRE AND SUMMARY OF MONTHLY INCOME AND EXPENSES

	App.	Spouse	Joint ✓

Proposal		Date _April 1, 1998_

Mr ⊙ Miss Mrs. Ms Family Name _JONES_	All Given Names _HAROLD WILLIAM_		
Mailing Address _21 MAIN STREET_	Town/City _TORONTO_	Province _ONT_	Postal Code _M5L 3T3_
Social Insurance No: _123-456-789_	Date of Birth: Day _30_ Month _09_ Year _1953_		
Married ✓	Single	Widow(er)	Divorced	Common Law	Separated

Business Phone #:	Home Phone #: _779-0007_	Message No:
Usual Occupation _SALESMAN_	Name of Present Employer _ABC SALES INC._	Since When
Address of Employer _7724 EAST ST., NORTH YORK, ONT._	If Unemployed - Since When	

Spouse's Name _MARY_		Spouses S.I.N. _987-654-321_
Spouse's Address _SAME_		
Spouse's Employer _UNEMPLOYED_	Position	Since When	If Unemployed, Since When
Spouse's Date of Birth: D _06_ M _02_ Y _1957_	Spouse Phone #: Res _SAME_	Bus

ALL DEPENDENTS WHO RELY ON YOU FOR FINANCIAL SUPPORT

Family & Given Names	Relationship	Date of Birth Day/Month/Year	Address (if different from applicant)	Income
HAROLD JR.	_S_	_12/9/84_		_NIL_
JENNIFER	_D_	_5/2/87_		_NIL_
JOSHUA	_S_	_21/8/91_		_NIL_

ALL EMPLOYERS FOR THE PAST TWO YEARS (In periods when drawing U.I.C. show each period separately)

Employer's Name	Employer's Address	Date Job or U.I. Started Ended
ABC SALES	_7724 EAST ST., NORTH YORK_	
UIC		
ABC SALES		

For which year was your last Tax Return filed? _1996_	Amount owing: _4,750_
What was your address when you filed that Return: _SAME_	Refund Received: _0_ Refund to Come:

RENT PAID - PAST CALENDAR YEAR

Address(es) of Principal Residence(s)	No. of Months Resident	Rent Paid	Property Tax Paid	Name of Landlord or Municipality to whom payment made

96

ASSETS

Estimated Value

Cash On Hand .... $ _____
Cash On Deposit   Bank: _____   Account No: _____   _____
                               Bank: _____   Account No: _____   _____
Furniture, Appliances .... _4,000_
Other Assets (Collections, musical instruments, furs, jewellery etc.)(Show details on Page.4) .... _2,000_
Securities (Stocks, bonds, R.R.S.P., cash value of Life Insurance) (Show details on Page.4) ....
Real Estate - House, Cottage, Land (show details on Page.4) .... _160,000_
Motorized and Recreational Vehicles : Include here details of cars, trucks, campers, trailers, boats, etc. .... _8,000_

Details	Licence No.	Year	Make	Serial No.
FORD SABLE	ABC 123	1996		

If you have borrowed money on any of the assets above, provide details below (attach copies of contracts and/or agreements):

Creditor's Name	Date Assets Pledged	Type of Asset Pledged	Present Amount of Loan	Present Value of Asset
FIRST BANK OF CANADA	SEPT./93	HOUSE	150,000	160,000
FORD CREDIT	JUNE /97	SABLE	6,000	8,000

If you have co-signed a loan or contract for anyone else, show details below:

Lender's Name	Address	Amount	Borrower's Name	Borrower's Address

Has anyone co-signed for you?   Yes _____   No _____.

Income (Monthly)

Take home pay of applicant from -   Employment _____   U.I.C. _____ $ _3,200_
                                       (Attach last Pay Stub)
Take Home Pay of Spouse .... _____
Allowances, Pensions, Alimony, etc. .... _____
Income from other sources (Specify) .... _____
                                                     Total: $ _3,200_

Monthly Expenses

~~Rent~~/Mortgage	$ _1,100_	Hair Salon	$	_40_
~~Taxes/Condo Fees~~	_250_	Car Insurance		_90_
Hydro/Phone/Fuel/Water	_255_	Monthly Car Payment		_250_
Telephone/Cable TV	_75_	Vehicle Operating Expense (Gas, Oil, etc.)		_125_
Home Insurance	_60_	Personal Travel		
Food	_350_	Prescription Drugs		_40_
Meals Outside Home	_100_	Laundry/Dry Cleaning		_35_
Drug Store		Gifts		
Clothing	_125_	Pet Expenses		
Babysitting/Day Care		Recreation		_100_
Magazines/Books/etc.	_25_	Childs Expense (Allowance School/etc.)		_100_
Donations		Personal Expense (Cigarettes/Alcohol/Entertainment)		_100_
Doctor/Dentist		Alimony/Maintenance		
Life Insurance		....		
Sub Total	$ _2,340_	Sub Total	$	_880_

TOTAL OF MONTHLY EXPENSES .... $ _3,220_

Are you behind in your Child Support?   Yes ____   No ____

If you paid alimony or maintenance payments during the past year: Amount paid was $_____ and was paid
to: _____
                                                                (name and address)

If the answer to any of the following questions is YES, please expand your answer

		YES	NO
1.	Have you been bankrupt before?	( )	(✓)
2.	Have you applied for assistance through Credit Counselling, Orderly Payment of debt, Court Consolidation, Voluntary Deposit	( )	(✓)
3.	Are you bonded in your present position?	( )	(✓)
4.	Have you received or do you expect to receive an inheritance?	( )	(✓)
5.	Are there any Writs, Judgements, Garnishments or Wage Assignments outstanding against you?	( )	(✓)
6.	Have you been self-employed in the last 5 years?	( )	(✓)
7.	Within the last 12 months have you:		
	(a) disposed of or transferred any of your assets?	( )	(✓)
	(b) made payments in excess of regular payments to a creditor?	( )	(✓)
	(c) had any assets seized by any creditor?	( )	(✓)
8.	Within the last 5 years have you:		
	(a) sold, disposed of or transferred any real estate?	( )	(✓)
	(b) made any gifts to relatives or others in excess of $500?	( )	(✓)
9.	Have you made arrangements to continue to pay any creditors?	( )	(✓)
10.	Do you have a safety deposit box? contains will, insurance papers	(✓)	( )
11.	Do you have any credit cards? — cards given to trustee	(✓)	( )
12.	Does your spouse have any assets?	( )	(✓)

Please describe briefly the circumstances which have caused your financial problems and tell us what collection actions creditors are now taking, and how you feel bankruptcy will help you.

I was unemployed for a long period in 1996/97 and built up debts. My wife and I are unable to catch up.

13. Please provide a telephone number where you can be contacted between the hours of 8:30am and 4:30pm:
(905) - 992 - 8999

" I hereby certify that the information contained in this application is true and complete in every respect and fully disclose the state of my affairs. In addition, any income in excess of reasonable cost of living will be paid to the Trustee."

April 1, 1998
Date

Harold W. Jones
Signature of Applicant

98

DEBTS

Complete Name of All Creditors	Complete Address of Creditor (including Postal Code)	Credit Card Account No.	Estimated Amount Owing		Reason for Debt
FIRST BANK OF CANADA	123 FIRST ST - MTL, QUE	8544793-888	150,000	joint	HOUSE MTGE
FORD CREDIT	1234S FORD DR - OAKVILLE, ONT	8949-7301-4901	6,000	Harold	car loan
FIRST BANK OF CANADA	123 FIRST ST, MONTREAL		10,477	joint	personal loan
FIRSTBANK VISA	2712 RUE D'OBLIGATIONS, QUEBEC, QUE	778-887-878	4,875	Harold	cr. card
JACK'S DISCOUNT CENTRE	78 ROSE ST, TORONTO		378.95	Mary	purchase
REVGIVUE CANADA	TAXATION CENTRES, 875 HERON RD, OTTAWA KIA 181	435-999-111	4,750	Harold	income tax
ROLAND J. REYNOLDS	653 FLUSHRON DR., TORONTO		8,000	Harold	personal loan
S.J.W. SMITH & Co	76498 SOUTHWEST DR. SAN FRANCISCO, CALIFORNIA ATTN: J. SOUTH		78.90	Mary	books
SUPERCARD	SUPERCARD BATH CENTRE, 7924 BRAMBLE DR., 23rd FLOOR, WILLOWDALE	543-6792-546-2378	2,754	joint	cr. card

```
District of
Division No.
Court No.      31-875539
               31-875540
Estate No.     31-875539
               31-875540
```

IN THE MATTER OF THE BANKRUPTCY OF

Harold William Jones and Mary Jones
of the City of Toronto in the Province of Ontario

INCOME AND EXPENSE STATEMENT

NET MONTHLY INCOME:

Net Salary	3,200.00	
TOTAL NET MONTHLY INCOME		3,200.00

MONTHLY EXPENSES:

Non-discretionary expenses:

Rent, Mortgage or Board Payment	1,100.00
Cable TV	75.00
Meals outside home	100.00
House - fire insurance & taxes	310.00
Hair salon, prescription drugs	80.00
Auto - Insurance and payments	250.00
Magazines, books, recreation	110.00
Children's allowance	100.00
Personal expenses - miscellaneous	100.00
Utilities - gas, hydro,water,phone	240.00
Food	350.00
Clothing	125.00

Discretionary expenses:

Payment being made to Trustee	100.00
Auto Operating Expenses	125.00
Laundry & Dry Cleaning	35.00

TOTAL MONTHLY EXPENSES	3,200.00

SURPLUS OR DEFICIT	0.00

Dated April 6, 1998

_____
Signature

It was clear from their questionnaire and summary of
monthly income and expenses that they did not have any
surplus income to commit to payments to creditors under
a proposal. They needed every cent just to get by. They
decided that they had to file an assignment in bankruptcy.
Mary had co-signed for the car loan, bank loan and credit
cards. Therefore, to get a fresh start, they both had to file

for bankruptcy protection. Since almost all their debts were the same, we were able to file a *joint bankruptcy*, a single estate that dealt with all their creditors together. Otherwise, if their debts were not the same, each would file for separate individual bankruptcies.

Before they filed the bankruptcy, we reviewed their assets and how I, as trustee, would be treating them in a bankruptcy.

1. Personal Possessions

They were entitled to keep their personal possessions because the resale value was less than $2,000 ($1,000 exemption per person). As trustee, I had no interest in these assets because their value was within the exempt limit.

2. Furniture

The total resale value of their used furniture was less than $4,000 and therefore they were entitled to claim the exemption of $2,000 per person. As trustee, I had no interest in this asset.

3. Automobile

The fair market value of the 1996 Mercury Sable, which I confirmed in the "Black Book" of prices, was about $8,000. The related secured debt owing to Ford Credit Canada Ltd. was about $6,000. Since Harold's sales job required driving from customer to customer, he needed his car to do his job. Therefore, he claimed the $2,000 remaining equity exempt as a *tool of his trade*. Again, as trustee, I had no interest in the car.

4. Real Estate

The estimated fair market value of their house had dropped to about $160,000. I confirmed this with an independent real estate agent. The bank's mortgage on the house was approximately $150,000. If the house were sold, after deducting the agent's commission and related legal costs, it is unlikely that more than $150,000 would be realized. I explained that in a situation like this, where the net realizable value and the mortgage are almost identical in amount, a trustee would not take any action to disturb the ownership.

We also reviewed their income and expenses and their obligations to make monthly payments during bankruptcy. The Joneses net family take-home pay was $3,200 per month. With five persons dependent on this income, based upon the superintendent's guidelines, we agreed to monthly payments of $100.00 over the nine months of bankruptcy.

Now, let's follow Harold and Mary through their actual bankruptcy process, looking at the various forms on pages 103–108.

ASSESSMENT CERTIFICATE

To: Superintendent of Bankruptcy

From: <u>Frank Sheldon Kisluk</u>
             Trustee or administrator of consumer proposal or
             individual conducting the assessment in a remote area

Re: Harold William Jones and Mary Jones

Date: <u>April 1, 1998</u>
             Date of assessment

I, the undersigned, hereby certify that I have complied with the Directive "Assessment of an Individual Debtor".

Dated at Toronto, this 6th day of April, 1998.

(signature)

Signature of trustee, administrator,
(Please check off box if the assessment was performed in a designated area or   ☐
pursuant to the extraordinary circumstances provision)

ACKNOWLEDGEMENT

We, the undersigned debtors, have consulted with the above-named individuals.

After having discussed our financial situation and the merits and consequences of each option available, we have decided on the following option.

☐ (a) a consumer proposal   ☐ (b) Division 1 proposal   ☑ (c) an assignment in bankruptcy

In the last six months we have **not** received any assessment of our financial situation   ☑
other than that referred to in this certificate.

– OR –

In the last six months we have received advice regarding our financial situation other   ☐
than the type of assessment referred to in this certificate.

If other advice was received indicate the amount paid: $_____.

Dated at Toronto, this 6th day of April, 1998.

(signature)

Signature of the debtors

(signature)

103

```
District of
Division No.
Court No.      31-875539
               31-875540
Estate No.     31-875539
```

31-875540

ASSIGNMENT
For the general benefit of creditors

```
Full legal names of debtors
     Jones    Harold William
     Jones    Mary
Family Name              First names
Address
                                                    Occupation
     21 Main Street                                 Salesman
     Toronto, Ont  M5L 3T3                           Unemployed
```

```
Name of Trustee

     MANDELBAUM SPERGEL INC.
```

We, being unable to pay our debts as they become due, hereby assign and abandon all our property to the trustee, for the general benefit of our creditors pursuant to the Act.

Signed at the City of Toronto in the Province of Ontario
in the presence of Frank Kisluk.

Witness	Date	Signature of Debtors
	April 6, 1998	

104

District of
Division No.
Court No.   31-875539
             31-875540
Estate No.   31-875539
             31-875540

STATEMENT OF AFFAIRS OF
NON-BUSINESS BANKRUPT

IN THE MATTER OF THE BANKRUPTCY OF
Harold William Jones and Mary Jones
of the City of Toronto in the Province of Ontario
(Summary Administration)

Type of Assets		Description (be specific)	Exempt property Yes	No	Estimated dollar value
1-Cash on hand					NIL
2-Furniture		Household furniture and effects	X		4000.00
3-Personal Effects		Personal effects	X		2000.00
4-Life Insurance Policies, RRSPs, etc.					NIL
5-Securities					NIL
6-Real Property	House	21 Main Street, Toronto (encumb.)		X	160000.00
	Cottage				NIL
	Land				NIL
7-Motorized Vehicle	Automobile	1996 Ford Sable (encumb.)	X		8000.00
	Motorcycle				NIL
	Snowmobile				NIL
	Other				NIL
8-Recreational Equipment					NIL
9-Estimated Tax Refund					NIL
10-Other Assets					NIL
		TOTAL			174000.00

April 6, 1998
Date

Bankrupt

105

STATEMENT OF AFFAIRS (LIABILITIES)

Harold William Jones and Mary Jones
(Summary Administration)

Creditor	Address	Account No.	Amount of Debt		
			Unsec.	Sec.	Pref.
First Bank of Canada	123 First Street Montreal, Que	8544893-888		150000.00	
Ford Credit	12348 Ford Drive Oakville, Ont	8749-7301-4985		6000.00	
First Bank of Canada (Personal Loans)	123 First Street Montreal, Que		10477.00		
Firstbank Visa	2712 Rue D'Obligations Quebec, Que	778-887-878	4875.00		
Jack's Discount Centre	78 Rose Street Toronto, Ont		378.00		
Revenue Canada	Taxation Centre 875 Heron Rd. Ottawa, Ont	435-999-111	4750.00		
Ronald J. Reynolds	653 Flushron Road Mississauga, Ont		8000.00		
S.J.M.Smith & Co. Ltd. Attn: J. South	76498 Southwest Drive San Francisco, Cal		80.00		
Supercard	Supercard Data Centre 7984 Bramble Dr., 23rd floor Willowdale, Ont	543-6798-546-2378	2754.00		

Details of Pledged Assets:
First Bank of Canada   -21 Main Street, Toronto
Ford Credit   -1996 Ford Sable

TOTAL Pref.	*********** *********** NIL
TOTAL Sec.	*********** 156000.00 ***********
TOTAL Unsec.	31314.00 *********** ***********
GRAND TOTAL	187314.00

April 6, 1998
Date

Bankrupt

106

STATEMENT OF AFFAIRS

PERTINENT INFORMATION RELATING TO THE AFFAIRS OF A BANKRUPT

(Summary Administration)

A- PERSONAL DATA

1-Family Name	Given Names	Date of Birth		
		Day	Mo.	Yr
Jones	Harold William	30	09	53
Jones	Mary	06	02	57

2-Also known as:

3-Complete address including Postal Code

21 Main Street

Toronto, Ont M5L 3T3

4-Marital Status

__X__ Married   ___Single   ___Widowed   ___Separated   ___Divorced   ___Common-Law

5-Name of Spouse in full

Mary Jones

6-Name of Present Employer	Occupation (Bankrupt)
ABC Sales Inc.	Salesman
	Unemployed

7-Dependents (as defined by the Income Tax Act)

Number aged 15 or less	Number from 16 to 21	Number of adults including spouse
2	1	1

Number of dependents residing with bankrupt (excluding bankrupt): 0

8-Have you operated a business within the last 5 years?	Yes	No	
		X	

B - WITHIN THE 12 MONTHS PRIOR TO THE DATE OF THE INITIAL BANKRUPTCY EVENT, HAVE YOU...

9A- Sold or disposed of any of your assets?	Yes	No	9B- Made payments in excess of regular payments to a creditor?	Yes	No	9C- Had any assets seized by any creditor?	Yes	No
		X			X			X

C - WITHIN FIVE YEARS PRIOR TO THE DATE OF THE INITIAL BANKRUPTCY EVENT, HAVE YOU...

10A-Disposed or transferred any real estate?	Yes	No	10B-Made any gifts to relatives or others in excess of $500?	Yes	No	10C-Made any arrangements to continue to pay any creditor?	Yes	No
		X			X			X

D - BUDGET INFORMATION

11-INCOME		12-EXPENSES	
A Total earnings	3200.00	A Fixed expenses	1650.00
B Contributions of others in the household	NIL	B Others	
		Laundry & Dry Cleaning	35.00
C Other earnings. (Specify)	NIL	Auto Operating Expenses	125.00
		Clothing	125.00
		Food	350.00
		Meals outside home	100.00

April 6, 1998

Date _____   Bankrupt _____

STATEMENT OF AFFAIRS

PERTINENT INFORMATION RELATING TO THE AFFAIRS OF A BANKRUPT

(Summary Administration)

		Auto - Insurance and payments	250.00
		Magazines, books, recreation	110.00
		Children's allowance	100.00
		Personal expenses - miscellaneous	100.00
		Hair salon, prescription drugs	80.00
		Cable TV	75.00
		C Payment being made to trustee	100.00
E - TOTAL INCOME	3200.00	F - TOTAL EXPENSES	3200.00

13-Have you been bankrupt before? ___ Yes _X_ No

14-If you answered Yes to question 13, when did you receive your absolute discharge?

15-Have you ever filed a proposal under the Bankruptcy and Insolvency Act? ___ Yes _X_ No

16-If you answered Yes to question 15, when did you file the proposal?

17-Give reasons for your financial difficulty.

18-If answers to any of questions 8,9,10,13 and 15 is yes, give details:

    We, the undersigned do swear that this statement is to the best of our knowledge a full, true and complete statement of our affairs on the 6th day of April 1998 and fully discloses all property of every description that is in our posession or that may devolve on us in accordance with section 67 of the Act.

Sworn before me at the City of Toronto
in the Province of Ontario
this 6th day of April 1998.

_____   _____

                                            Bankrupt

NOTICE TO CREDITORS

The creditors received the notice on page 109, together with a copy of the statement of affairs and a form to file their claim with the trustee's office. As you can see, because they are first-time bankrupts, if no one opposes their discharge, they will be automatically discharged on the date shown in the notice.

```
District of
Division No.
Court No.   31-875539
            31-875540
Estate No.  31-875539
            31-875540
```

**NOTICE OF BANKRUPTCY AND OF IMPENDING AUTOMATIC DISCHARGE OF
FIRST-TIME BANKRUPT AND TO REQUEST A FIRST MEETING OF CREDITORS**
IN THE MATTER OF THE BANKRUPTCY OF
Harold William Jones
and Mary Jones
of the City of Toronto in the Province of Ontario
(Summary Administration)

Take notice that:

1.   Harold   William   Jones   and   Mary   Jones   filed an assignment in
bankruptcy on April 6th, 1998, and the undersigned MANDELBAUM SPERGEL
INC. were appointed as trustee of the estate of the bankrupts by the
official receiver, subject to the affirmation by the creditors of the
trustee's appointment or the substitution of another trustee by the
creditors.

2. Pursuant to paragraph 155(d.1) of the Act a first meeting of creditors
will be required only if within thirty days after the date of bankruptcy,
the official receiver or creditors who have in aggregate at least twenty
five percent in value of the proven claims request a meeting to be held.

3. To request such a meeting and to vote at a meeting, a creditor must
lodge with the trustee before such request for a meeting, a proof of claim
and, where necessary, a proxy.

4. Enclosed with this notice is a form of proof of claim, a form of proxy
and a list of creditors with claims amounting to twenty five dollars or
more, showing the amounts of their claims.

5. Also enclosed pursuant to paragraph 102(3) of the Act is information
concerning the financial situation of the bankrupts and the obligation of
the bankrupts to make payments to the estate of the bankrupts, as required
under Section 68 of the Act.

6. Creditors must prove their claims against the estate of the bankrupts
in order to share in any distribution of the proceeds realized from the
estate.

7. Pursuant to section 168.1 of the Bankruptcy and Insolvency Act, the
bankrupts, being an individual who has never before been bankrupt, will
be given an automatic discharge on the 6th day of January, 1999 unless
the Superintendent of Bankruptcy, the trustee of the estate of the
bankrupts, or a creditor of the bankrupts gives notice of intended
opposition to the discharge of the bankrupts before that date.

8. Any creditor who intends to oppose the discharge of the bankrupts shall
state in writing the grounds for their opposition, and send a notice to
this effect to Division Office, the trustee of the estate of the
bankrupts, and the bankrupts at any time before the 6th day of January,
1999.

9.   Where any creditor opposes the discharge of the bankrupt, a court fee
applies.

10. Where the discharge of the bankrupts is opposed, the trustee will
apply to the Court without delay for an appointment for the hearing of the
opposition in the manner prescribed by the Act unless it is a matter to be
dealt with through mediation pursuant to Section 170.1(4) of the Act.

DATED AT Toronto, Ontario this 10th day of April, 1998.

```
MANDELBAUM SPERGEL INC. - Trustee
505 Consumers Road, Suite 201
Toronto, Ontario
M2J 4V8
```

A CREDITOR'S CLAIM

An example of one of the claims filed in the Joneses' bankruptcy is shown on page 111. Even though creditors were listed on the statement of affairs by the Joneses, they must still file a *proof of claim* with the trustee in order to be able to vote at the creditors' meeting.

PROOF OF CLAIM

(see reverse for instructions)

IN THE MATTER OF THE BANKRUPTCY (~~OR PROPOSAL OR RECEIVERSHIP OF THE PROPERTY~~) OF

HAROLD   WILLIAM   JONES _____(referred to in this form as "the debtor")

(name of debtor)

and the claim of   FIRSTBANK   VISA _____(referred to in this form as "the creditor")

(name of creditor)

All notices or correspondence regarding this claim to be forwarded to the creditor at the following address: _____

2712 RUE D'Obligations, Quebec City, Quebec

Telephone: _____ Fax: _____

I, Jean Jolie _____, residing in the   city

(name of person signing claim)   (city, town, etc.)

of   Quebec _____ in the Province of   Quebec

(name of city, town, etc.)

Do hereby certify that:

1. ☐ I am the creditor

If an officer of the company, state position or title

☑ or I am   COLLECTION   OFFICER _____ of the creditor.

(state position or title)

2. I have knowledge of all the circumstances connected with the claim referred to in this form.

The statement of account must specify the vouchers or other evidence in support of the claim

3. The debtor was at the date of the bankruptcy ~~(or the proposal or the receivership)~~, namely the   6th   day of   April   19~~76~~, and still is indebted to the creditor in the sum of $ 4,875   as shown by the statement of account attached hereto and marked "Schedule A", after deducting any counter claims to which the debtor is entitled.

Check and complete appropriate category

4. A ☑ Unsecured claim. In respect to the said debt, the creditor does not hold any assets of the debtor as security and:

Check appropriate description

(i) ☑ does not claim a right to a priority.

Set out on an attached schedule details to support priority claim

or

(ii) ☐ claims a right to a priority under section 136 of the Bankruptcy and Insolvency Act.

Give full particulars of the security, including the date on which the security was given and the value at which the creditor assesses the security, and attach a copy of the security documents

B ☐ Secured claim. In respect of the said debt, the creditor holds assets of the debtor valued at $ _____ as security, particulars of which are as follows:

Attach a copy of sales agreement and delivery documents

C ☐ Claim by farmer, fisherman, or aquaculturist. The creditor hereby makes a claim under subsection 81.2(1) of the Bankruptcy and Insolvency Act for the unpaid amount of $_____

Strike out "is" or "is not"

5. To the best of my knowledge and belief, the creditor is/is not related to the debtor within the meaning of section 4 of the Bankruptcy and Insolvency Act.

Attach a separate schedule if necessary

6. The following are the payments that the creditor has received from and the credits that the creditor has allowed to the debtor within the three months (or, if the creditor and the debtor are related within the meaning of section 4 of the Bankruptcy and Insolvency Act, within the twelve months) immediately preceding the date of bankruptcy, proposal or receivership:

_____

_____

_____

Insert city and date of signature

Dated at   Quebec _____, this   20   day of   April _____, 19 98

Must be signed and witnessed

_____
Witness

_____
(signature of individual completing this form)

Warning: A trustee may, pursuant to subsection 128(3) of the Bankruptcy and Insolvency Act, redeem a security on payment to the secured creditor of the debt or the value of the security as assessed, in the proof of security, by the secured creditor.

Subsection 201(1) of the Bankruptcy and Insolvency Act provides severe penalties for making any false claim, declaration or statement of account.

See General Proxy on reverse

111

CREDITORS' MEETING

No creditor requested a meeting. After 30 days, Harold and Mary came to my office to deal with administrative matters. Harold brought in his last pay stub so that we could prepare the pre-bankruptcy income tax return and provided us with a set of postdated cheques to cover the required monthly payments.

COUNSELLING

Copies of the certificates are shown on pages 114–115. A bankrupt must attend these sessions in order to be eligible for an automatic discharge.

FIRST STAGE

File number 31-875539
31-875540

To: **Superintendent of Bankruptcy**

From: Frank Sheldon Kisluk
       Name of qualified counsellor

Re: Harold William Jones and Mary Jones

Date: June 4, 1998
       Date of counselling

I, the undersigned, hereby certify that I have complied with the
terms of Section 7 of the Counselling Directive.

Dated at Toronto, this 4th day of June, 1998.

_____

Signature of qualified counsellor

ACKNOWLEDGEMENT

We, the undersigned, have attended an individual session presented
by the above-mentioned qualified counsellor and understand the
information which was presented to us.

Dated at Toronto, this 4th day of June, 1998.

_____

Signature of bankrupts

114

COUNSELLING CERTIFICATE

SECOND STAGE

File number 31-875539
31-875540

To: **Superintendent of Bankruptcy**

From: Frank Sheldon Kisluk
      Name of qualified counsellor

Re: Harold William Jones and Mary Jones

Date: October 2, 1998
      Date of counselling

I, the undersigned, hereby certify that I have complied with the terms
of Section 8 of the Counselling Directive.

Dated at Toronto, this 2nd day of October, 1998.

_____

Signature of qualified counsellor

ACKNOWLEDGEMENT

We, the undersigned, have consulted with the above-named qualified
counsellor and acknowledge receiving and understanding the
counselling referred to in this certificate.

Dated at Toronto, this 2nd day of October, 1998.

_____

Signature of bankrupts

AUTOMATIC DISCHARGE

In November 1998, we confirmed that Harold and Mary's financial position had not materially changed from when they filed bankruptcy.

No creditor objected to the automatic discharge, and therefore, effective January 6, 1999, nine months after the filing date, I issued the *certificate of discharge* for Harold and Mary's bankruptcy (see page 117) and sent them a copy. Their bankruptcy was over.

```
District of
Division No.
Court No.   31-875539
            31-875540
Estate No.  31-875539
            31-875540
```

CERTIFICATE OF DISCHARGE

IN THE MATTER OF THE BANKRUPTCY OF
Harold William Jones
and Mary Jones
of the City of Toronto in the Province of Ontario
(Summary Administration)

Date of Bankruptcy: April 6, 1998

We, MANDELBAUM SPERGEL INC., the trustee of the estate of Harold William Jones and Mary Jones, bankrupts, hereby certify that, pursuant to subsection 168.1 of the Act, on the 6th day of January, 1999 the bankrupts is discharged and released from all debts except those matters referred to in subsection 178(1) of the Act.

DATED AT Toronto, Ontario, this 10th of January, 1999.

MANDELBAUM SPERGEL INC. - TRUSTEE

Per:

_____

117

TAX RETURNS

In March 1999, Harold brought in his 1998 T-4 and related tax slips. We filed an income tax return for him for the post-bankruptcy period of April 6 to December 31, 1998. This return resulted in a refund, which was paid into the bankruptcy estate, available for distribution to their creditors.

TRUSTEE'S FINAL STATEMENT

In June 1999, we received the refund for the post-bankruptcy income tax return and thereafter, prepared the *final statement of receipts and disbursements* (see pages 119–120). That statement is shown along with the schedule of final payments to creditors or *dividend distribution* (see pages 121–122). After payment of the dividends, we obtained our discharge as trustee and closed our file.

```
District of
Division No.
Court No.      31-875539
               31-875540
Estate No.     31-875539
               31-875540
```

IN THE MATTER OF THE BANKRUPTCY OF

Harold William Jones and Mary Jones

of the City of Toronto in the Province of Ontario

(Summary Administration)

TRUSTEE'S STATEMENT OF RECEIPTS AND DISBURSEMENTS

DRAFT

RECEIPTS

1. Miscellaneous					
Payment by bankrupt		$	900.00		
Pre-bankruptcy tax return			897.50		
Post-bankruptcy tax return			1,722.70		
Interest			12.50	$	3,532.70
	TOTAL RECEIPTS			$	3,532.70

DISBURSEMENTS

1. Fees Paid					
Fees paid Official Receiver - Filing fees		$	50.00	$	50.00
2. Trustee's remuneration					
Counselling fees			170.00		
G.S.T. on counselling fees			11.90		181.90

Administrative Disbursement	$100.00	

Trustee's Fees:			
100% of	$975.00	$975.00	
35% of	$1,025.00	$358.75	
50% of	$1,532.70	$766.35	

TOTAL REMUNERATION		2,200.10	
G.S.T. ON TRUSTEE'S REMUNERATION		154.01	
TOTAL TRUSTEE'S REMUNERATION AND G.S.T.			2,354.11
	TOTAL DISBURSEMENTS	$	2,586.01
AMOUNT AVAILABLE FOR DISTRIBUTION		$	946.69

==============
...\2

119

```
District of
Division No.
Court No.    31-875539
             31-875540
Estate No.   31-875539
             31-875540
```

TRUSTEE'S STATEMENT OF RECEIPTS AND DISBURSEMENTS   PAGE 2
IN THE MATTER OF THE BANKRUPTCY OF
Harold William Jones and Mary Jones

```
LEVY PAYABLE UNDER SECTION 147           $        47.33
UNSECURED CREDITORS -
   Proved Claims of       $    31,314.00
   Dividend                      946.69     3.02%
      less levy                   47.33        899.36
```

                                              $ 946.69
                                              ==============

NOTE:

1. BANKRUPT'S DISCHARGE
THE BANKRUPT RECEIVED AN AUTOMATIC DISCHARGE ON
JANUARY 6, 1999.

                            MANDELBAUM SPERGEL INC. - TRUSTEE
                            Per:

DATE 15 JUNE 1999   _____

District of
Division No.
Court No.   31-875539   / 31-875540
Estate No.   31-875539   / 31-875540

DIVIDEND SHEET

IN THE MATTER OF THE BANKRUPTCY OF

Harold William Jones and Mary Jones
of the City of Toronto in the Province of Ontario

(Summary Administration)

	Claim	Total Dividend	Total Levy	Total Payment	Interim Payment	Payment
UNSECURED						
First Bank of Canada (Personal Loans)	10477.00	316.74	15.84	300.90	0.00	300.90
123 First Street						
Montreal Que						
Firstbank Visa	4875.00	147.38	7.37	140.01	0.00	140.01
2712 Rue D'Obligations						
Quebec Que						
(Acct.# 778-887-878)						
Jack's Discount Centre	378.00	11.43	0.57	10.86	0.00	10.86
78 Rose Street						
Toronto Ont						
Revenue Canada	4750.00	143.60	7.18	136.42	0.00	136.42
Taxation Centre						
875 Heron Rd.						
Ottawa Ont						
(Acct.# 435-999-111)						
Ronald J. Reynolds	8000.00	241.86	12.09	229.77	0.00	229.77
653 Flushron Road						
Mississauga Ont						
S.J.M.Smith & Co. Ltd.	80.00	2.42	0.12	2.30	0.00	2.30
76498 Southwest Drive						
San Francisco Cal						
Supercard	2754.00	83.26	4.16	79.10	0.00	79.10
Supercard Data Centre						
7984 Bramble Dr., 23rd floor						
Willowdale Ont						
(Acct.# 543-6798-546-2378)						
TOTALS	$ 31314.00 $	946.69 $	47.33 $	899.36 $	0.00 $	899.36

121

```
District of
Division No.
Court No.    31-875539      / 31-875540
Estate No.   31-875539      / 31-875540
```

IN THE MATTER OF THE BANKRUPTCY OF

Harold William Jones and Mary Jones
of the City of Toronto in the Province of Ontario

(Summary Administration)

	Claim	Total Dividend	Total Levy	Total Payment	Interim Payment	Payment
GRAND TOTALS	$ 31314.00	$ 946.69	$ 47.33	$ 899.36	$ 0.00	$ 899.36

How did the creditors fare at the end? You can see that although the payments made to the creditors were not very large, all the unsecured creditors were treated equally.

Meanwhile, how did bankruptcy affect Harold, Mary and their children? After our first visit, Mary returned home to find a registered letter from a lawyer writing on behalf of the bank. Mary called the lawyer and told him that she and Harold were going to file bankruptcy with our office. The lawyer did not call again. Collectors called regarding the credit cards. Again, after being informed of the bankruptcy, they did not call again. The immediate effect of the bankruptcy filing is to put all the creditors into the same position, represented by the trustee. There is no purpose in pursuing collection if those efforts will be stopped by a bankruptcy.

After filing bankruptcy, the Joneses found that they were

able to make their car loan and house mortgage payments on time and could meet other day-to-day obligations. They discussed their bankruptcy with the bank and with Ford Credit. Both creditors were willing to continue with their secured loans and were pleased that the Joneses wished to continue.

As well, they were able to allocate small allowances for their children, and they actually began to put aside $50 per month into a savings account against emergencies.

They tell me now that the stress is gone, that they are much more relaxed with each other and that they take greater pleasure in being together as a family. Harold's sales are increasing and he is being considered for a management position, with a related salary increase.

Case Study 2

ROBERT SMITH:
A CONSUMER PROPOSAL

Let's suppose, for this example, that Robert and Janet Smith
have one child, aged three. Their only assets are protected from seizure by the Ontario Executions Act. Here is
their schedule of monthly income and expenses:

Income	3,200
Expenses	
Mortgage, taxes	1,350
Utilities	175
Car loan	250
Car expenses (gas, repairs, insurance)	205
Food and household items	350
Meals outside home	100
Clothing	125
Telephone, cable	50
Other (recreation, holidays etc.)	300
	2,905
Surplus	295

In order to avoid bankruptcy, the Smiths would like to
settle their debts with their unsecured creditors. All debts
are in Robert's name except the mortgage on their con-
dominium. The condo is, and always has been, owned
by Janet, and Robert has guaranteed the mortgage.

Robert's unsecured debts total $42,500. In addition, he has guaranteed the condo mortgage of $120,000. Robert feels confident that he can afford to pay $250 per month toward a settlement with his creditors. I explained the way in which a consumer proposal could be presented to his creditors; Robert agreed to offer a proposal to pay $250 per month for three years. Robert's proposal is shown on page 126.

CANADA

Province of Ontario
ESTATE NO. 31-112233

CONSUMER PROPOSAL
IN THE MATTER OF THE CONSUMER PROPOSAL OF
Robert Smith
of the City of Scarborough in the Province of Ontario

I, Robert Smith, a consumer debtor, hereby make the following consumer proposal under the Bankruptcy and Insolvency Act:

1. Payment of the claims of secured creditors shall be made in the following manner:

    Secured creditors will be paid as per the existing terms and conditions of their debt.

2. Payment of all claims directed by the said Bankruptcy and Insolvency Act to be paid in   priority to other claims in the distribution of my property shall be made in the following manner:

    There are no claims carrying this priority.

3. Payment of the fees and expenses of the administrator and payment of the fees and expenses of any person in respect of counselling shall be made in the following manner:

    The fees and expenses of the administrator shall be paid in priority to distributions to creditors at the rates prescribed by statute.

4. I shall make the following payments to MANDELBAUM SPERGEL INC., the administrator of the consumer proposal, for the benefit of the unsecured creditors:

    Monthly payments of $250 per month for a period of 36 months.

5. The administrator shall distribute the moneys received from me to the unsecured creditors in accordance with the following schedule:

    Distributions to crediors shall be made every twelve months.

    Dated at Toronto, Ontario this 15th day of April, 1998.

_____   _____
Witness   Consumer Debtor

This proposal was mailed to all unsecured creditors with the *notice to creditors*, the *statement of affairs*, and *voting letter* (see pages 128–134). If, within 45 days, no one objects or requests a meeting, a consumer proposal is considered approved by the creditors.

In this case, no creditor objected and a *notice of status of consumer proposal* (see page 135) was sent to the creditors, and Robert began making monthly payments to us.

CANADA
ESTATE NO. 31-112233

NOTICE TO CREDITORS OF CONSUMER PROPOSAL
IN THE MATTER OF THE CONSUMER PROPOSAL OF
Robert Smith of the City of Scarborough in the Province of Ontario

Take notice that:

1. Robert Smith, a consumer debtor, made a consumer proposal under section 66.13 of the Bankruptcy and Insolvency Act on the 15th day of April, 1998, and a copy of the consumer proposal was filed with the official receiver by me, Frank Sheldon Kisluk, the administrator of the consumer proposal on the 15th day of April, 1998.

2. Attached to this notice are the following documents:

    (a)   a copy of the consumer proposal
    (b)   a copy of the report of the administrator on the consumer proposal
    that was filed with the official receiver on the 15th day of April, 1998
    (c)   a form of proof of claim

3. As administrator, I will be required to call a meeting of creditors only if, pursuant to Sec. 66.15 of the Act,

    (a)   I am directed to do so by the official receiver within the 45 day period
    following the filing of the consumer proposal
    (b)   at the expiration of the 45 day period following the filing of the
    consumer proposal, creditors having in aggregate at least 25 percent of proven   claims
have so requested

4.   Any creditor who has proved a claim and who indicates dissent from the consumer   proposal to me prior to the expiration of the 45 day period following the filing of the   consumer proposal shall be deemed to have requested a meeting of creditors.

5.   If, within that 45 day period, I am not required to call a meeting of creditors, the consumer proposal shall, by virtue of subsection 66.18(1) of the Act be deemed to have been accepted by the creditors.

6.   In the event that the consumer proposal has been accepted or is deemed to have been accepted by the creditors, I will apply to the Court to review the consumer proposal only if pursuant to section 66.22 of the Act, I am requested to do so by the Official Receiver or any other interested party within 15 days after the day of acceptance or deemed acceptance of the consumer proposal.

7.   If within that 15 day period mentioned in paragraph 6 I am not requested to apply to the Court to review the consumer proposal, the consumer proposal is deemed to be approved by the Court.

Dated at Toronto, Ontario this 17th day of April, 1998.

MANDELBAUM SPERGEL INC.

PER:_____

STATEMENT OF AFFAIRS OF
NON-BUSINESS DEBTOR

IN THE MATTER OF THE PROPOSAL OF

Robert Smith

of the City of Scarborough in the Province of   Ontario

Type of Assets		**ASSETS** Description (be specific)	Exempt property Yes	No	Estimated dollar value
1-Cash on hand					NIL
2-Furniture		Household furniture and effects	X		2000.00
3-Personal Effects		Personal effects	X		1000.00
4-Life Insurance Policies, RRSPs, etc.					NIL
5-Securities					NIL
6-Real Property	House				NIL
	Cottage				NIL
	Land				NIL
7-Motorized Vehicle	Automobile	1993 Chevrolet (encumb.)		X	7500.00
	Motorcycle				NIL
	Snowmobile				NIL
	Other				NIL
8-Recreational Equipment					NIL
9-Estimated Tax Refund					NIL
10-Other Assets					NIL
		TOTAL			10500.00

April 15, 1998

Date   Debtor

STATEMENT OF AFFAIRS (LIABILITIES)

Robert Smith

Creditor	Address	Account No.	Amount of Debt Unsec.	Amount of Debt Sec.	Amount of Debt Pref.
GMAC				6500.00	
Canadian Sales Co.			1500.00		
Computer Book Club			750.00		
First Canadian Bank			15000.00		
First Candian Mortgage Corp			120000.00		
Japon Inmar			550.00		
Shoppers' Visa			3500.00		
Stephen Smither			20000.00		
Value Credit			1200.00		

Details of Pledged Assets:
GMAC   -1993 Chevrolet

TOTAL Pref.	***********	***********	NIL
TOTAL Sec.	***********	6500.00	***********
TOTAL Unsec.	162500.00	***********	***********
GRAND TOTAL			169000.00

April 15, 1998
Date   Debtor

130

STATEMENT OF AFFAIRS

PERTINENT INFORMATION RELATING TO THE AFFAIRS OF A DEBTOR

A- PERSONAL DATA

1-Family Name	Given Names	Date of Birth		
		Day	Mo.	Yr
Smith	Robert	07	12	62

2-Also known as:

3-Complete address including Postal Code
76 South Street, Suite 1220
Scarborough, Ont M2G 7C9

4-Marital Status

X Married   ___Single   ___Widowed   ___Separated   ___Divorced   ___Common-Law

5-Name of Spouse in full

6-Name of Present Employer	Occupation (Debtor)
Mogul Computers	Computer Analyst

7-Dependents (as defined by the Income Tax Act)

Number aged 15 or less	Number from 16 to 21	Number of adults including spouse
1	0	1

Number of dependents residing with bankrupt (excluding bankrupt): 0

8-Have you operated a business within the last 5 years?	Yes	No
		X

B - WITHIN THE 12 MONTHS PRIOR TO THE DATE OF THE INITIAL BANKRUPTCY EVENT, HAVE YOU...

9A- Sold or disposed of any of your assets?	Yes	No	9B- Made payments in excess of regular payments to a creditor?	Yes	No	9C- Had any assets seized by any creditor?	Yes	No
		X			X			X

C - WITHIN FIVE YEARS PRIOR TO THE DATE OF THE INITIAL BANKRUPTCY EVENT, HAVE YOU...

10A-Disposed or transferred any real estate?	Yes	No	10B-Made any gifts to relatives or others in excess of $500?	Yes	No	10C-Made any arrangements to continue to pay any creditor?	Yes	No
		X			X			X

D - BUDGET INFORMATION

11-INCOME		12-EXPENSES	
A Total earnings	3200.00	A Fixed expenses	1525.00
B Contributions of others in the household	NIL	B Others	
		Miscellaneous	300.00
C Other earnings. (Specify)	NIL	Auto Operating Expenses	205.00
		Telephone	50.00
		Clothing	125.00
		Food	350.00
		Car payments	250.00

April 15, 1998
Date   Debtor

131

STATEMENT OF AFFAIRS
PERTINENT INFORMATION RELATING TO THE AFFAIRS OF A DEBTOR

		Meals outside home	100.00
		C Payment being made to trustee	250.00
E - TOTAL INCOME	3200.00	F - TOTAL EXPENSES	3155.00

13-Have you been bankrupt before?   ___ Yes   X No

14-If you answered Yes to question 13, when did you receive your absolute discharge?

15-Have you ever filed a proposal under the Bankruptcy and Insolvency Act?   ___ Yes   X No

16-If you answered Yes to question 15, when did you file the proposal?

17-Give reasons for your financial difficulty.

Robert Smith is unable to maintain payments to all of his cr
editors

18-If answers to any of questions 8,9,10,13 and 15 is yes, give details:

I, the undersigned do swear that this statement is to the best of my knowledge a full, true
and complete statement of my affairs on the 15th day of April 1998 and fully discloses all property of every
description that is in my possession or that may devolve on me in accordance with section 67 of the Act.

Sworn before me at the City of Toronto
in the Province of Ontario
this 15th day of April 1998.

_____   _____
                                                      Debtor

132

```
District of
Division No.
Court No.    31-112233
Estate No.   31-112233
```

IN THE MATTER OF THE PROPOSAL OF

Robert Smith
of the City of Scarborough in the Province of
Ontario

INCOME AND EXPENSE STATEMENT

NET MONTHLY INCOME:

Net Salary	3,200.00	
TOTAL NET MONTHLY INCOME		3,200.00

MONTHLY EXPENSES:

Non-discretionary expenses:		
Rent, Mortgage or Board Payment	1,100.00	
Taxes	250.00	
Hydro, water, gas	175.00	
Food	350.00	
Meals outside home	100.00	
Clothing	125.00	
Discretionary expenses:		
Telephone	50.00	
Payment being made to Trustee	250.00	
Car payments	250.00	
Auto Operating Expenses	205.00	
Miscellaneous	300.00	
TOTAL MONTHLY EXPENSES		3,155.00
SURPLUS OR DEFICIT		45.00

```
Dated April 15, 1998              _____
                                          Signature
```

District of
Division No.
COURT NO: 31-112233
ESTATE NO: 31-112233

VOTING LETTER
(Paragraphs 51 (1) (f) and 66.15 (3) (c)

IN THE MATTER OF THE PROPOSAL OF
Robert Smith
of the City of Scarborough in the Province of Ontario

I, _____

of _____

a creditor in the above matter for the sum of $ _____ ,

hereby request the trustee acing with respect of the proposal to record my vote FOR/AGAINST

the acceptance of the consumer proposal as made on the 15th of April, 1998.

Dated at _____, _____

this _____ day of _____, 19____.

_____   _____
Signature of witness   Signature of creditor

_____   _____
Signature of witness   Name of Title of Signing Officer

134

```
District of
Division No.
Court No.  31-112233
Estate No. 31-112233
```

NOTICE OF STATUS OF CONSUMER PROPOSAL
(Section 66.27))

IN THE MATTER OF THE CONSUMER PROPOSAL OF

Robert Smith
of the City of Scarborough in the Province of   Ontario

Take   notice   that   the   consumer   proposal of Robert Smith ,
a consumer debtor, made on the 15th of April, 1998, a copy of which
was   filed with the Official Receiver on the 15th of April, 1998, has
been accepted or deemed to be accepted by the creditors of   the
consumer debtor.

Dated at Toronto, Ontario this 30th of May, 1998.

MANDELBAUM SPERGEL INC.
Per:

Over the course of three years, we will distribute money
to the creditors annually. At the end of the three years,
after completing the payments, Robert will receive from
my office a *certificate of full performance* (see page 136).
This document confirms that he has made all payments
as agreed and therefore has no further obligations to his
proposal creditors.

LIFE AFTER DEBT

```
District of
Division No.
Court No.   31-112233
Estate No. 31-112233
```

CERTIFICATE OF FULL PERFORMANCE OF CONSUMER PROPOSAL
(Section 66.38)

IN THE MATTER OF THE CONSUMER PROPOSAL OF

Robert Smith
of the City of Scarborough in the Province of   Ontario

We, MANDELBAUM SPERGEL INC., administrator of the consumer proposal of Robert Smith   , a consumer debtor, hereby certify that the consumer debtor has, as of the 15th day of April, 2001 fully performed the provisions of the consumer debtor's proposal, as filed with the Official Receiver on the 15th day of April, 1998 .

Dated at Toronto, Ontario this 15th day of April, 2001.

MANDELBAUM SPERGEL INC.
Per:

_____

After the final payment to the creditors, we will prepare our *final statement of receipts and disbursements* (see Case Study 1). We will then complete our paperwork and close the file.

Case Study 3
JACK GREENE:
AN ORDINARY PROPOSAL

Jack Greene is a salaried lawyer employed by Empire Development Corporation. He is married with two young children and earns $100,000 per year. Although he has always managed his finances carefully, during the past several years he has been facing increasing financial pressure.

In October 1994, Jack borrowed $100,000 as a second mortgage on his Toronto home (which had always been held in his wife's name). He invested that amount in a business venture, Sure Thing Inc., with his old friend Jeremy. Jeremy ran the business and Jack collected monthly payments from the business to pay the additional mortgage payments on the $100,000 loan. Unfortunately, the business failed in February 1996, and Jack was left with the second mortgage and its $1,000 monthly payment, but with no more income from the business.

To make matters worse, the business had borrowed $300,000 from the bank, a loan which was personally guaranteed by both Jack and Jeremy. After the business failed, the bank, as a secured creditor, sold all the business assets and still had an outstanding balance due of $120,000. The bank demanded payment from both Jack and Jeremy as guarantors. Jeremy, without a job or assets, filed personal bankruptcy. The bank sued Jack for the total amount.

It was at this time that Jack met with me. Here is how we dealt with his problems.

Jack and I reviewed his statement of monthly family income and expenses:

Income (after income taxes)	5,500
Expenses	
Mortgage, property taxes	3,000
Utilities	250
Car loan payments	250
Car expenses (gas, repairs, insurance)	250
Food and household expenses	400
Meals outside home	150
Clothing	200
Telephone, cable	75
Health club	50
Vacation	250
Sundry	100
	4,975
Surplus	525

He listed his family assets and liabilities as follows:

WIFE'S ASSETS		
House	Fair market value	325,000
Deduct: Mortgages	First mortgage	200,000
	Second mortgage (re business loan)	100,000
	Total Mortgages	300,000
	Net equity in house	25,000

JACK'S ASSETS & LIABILITIES		
Assets		
Car 1		3,000
Car 2	Fair market value 10,000	
	Deduct: car loan 8,000	2,000
RRSP		7,000
	Total Assets	12,000
Liabilities		
Direct Debt		
Credit cards (six cards)		25,000
Personal loan from friend A		50,000
Personal loan from friend B		25,000
Guarantee to bank on failed business loan		120,000
		220,000
Contingent Debt		
Guarantee of house first mortgage		200,000
Guarantee of house second mortgage		100,000
		300,000
	Total Debt	520,000

It was obvious from Jack's statement of income and expenses that he could not service all of his direct debts from his income. (His contingent debts were only guarantees on the secured house mortgages and did not require any payments other than the regular mortgage payments.)

Jack's *surplus* income of $525 per month was not even enough to pay interest at ten percent on the direct debt. That alone would require after-tax surplus income of $22,000 per year or $1,833 per month!

Jack wanted to keep his cars and RRSP and avoid bankruptcy, concerned that it would reflect poorly on his personal reputation as a lawyer.

Based on Jack's realistic budget, we agreed that a monthly payment of $500 could be offered to creditors. As well, we felt that four years of payments would indicate Jack's best intentions to his creditors.

Since the bank was about to obtain judgment the next day and possibly garnish his wages, we had to move quickly. That same day, January 16, 1997, Jack filed a *notice of intention to make a proposal* (see page 141). I immediately filed this with Industry Canada, Bankruptcy Division, and provided a copy to both the bank's lawyer and to the court, thus stopping their action until a proposal could be filed and voted on. The notice was also mailed to all creditors.

CANADA
Province of Ontario

ESTATE NO: 31-855992
COURT NO: 31-855992

NOTICE OF INTENTION TO MAKE A PROPOSAL
(Subsection 50.4 (1)

IN THE MATTER OF THE PROPOSAL OF

Jack Greene
of the City of Toronto in the Province of Ontario

Take notice that:

1. I, Jack Greene an insolvent person, pursuant to subsection 50.4 (1) of the Bankruptcy and Insolvency Act, intent to make a proposal to my creditors.

2. Frank Sheldon Kisluk, of Mandelbaum Spergel Inc., of Toronto, Ontario, a licensed trustee, has consented to act as trustee under the proposal and a copy of the consent is attached hereto.

3. A list of the names of the known creditors with claims amounting to $250.00 or more and the amounts of their claims is attached.

4. Pursuant to section 69 of the Bankruptcy and Insolvency Act, all proceedings against me are stayed as of the date of filing this notice with the Official Receiver in my locality.

Dated at Toronto, Ontario this 16th of January, 1997.

_____
Insolvent Person

_____

To be completed by Official Receiver

Filing Date: _____

_____
Official Receiver

Jack immediately stopped paying all his unsecured creditors. He prepared his *statement of projected cash flow* (see page 142) which was filed through our office within ten days of the filing of the notice of intent. We then prepared the proposal (see pages 143–144).

IN THE MATTER OF THE PROPOSAL OF
JACK GREENE

STATEMENT OF PROJECTED CASH FLOW

		FEB/97	MARCH/97
INCOME	Net salary	5,500	5,500
EXPENSES			
	Mortgage	2,700	2,700
	Taxes	300	300
	Meals outside home	150	150
	Food	400	400
	Clothing	200	200
	Heat, light, power	250	250
	Telephone	75	75
	Car loan payments	250	250
	Auto operating expenses	250	250
	Health club	50	50
	Miscellaneous	350	350
TOTAL MONTHLY EXPENSES		4,975	4,975
EXCESS OF INCOME OVER EXPENSES		525	525

Dated January 26, 1997   _____

Jack Greene

PROPOSAL

In the Matter of the Proposal of **Jack Greene** of the City of
North York, in the Municipality of Metropolitan Toronto
in the Province of Ontario

Jack Greene, the above named debtor, hereby submits the following
proposal under the Bankruptcy and Insolvency Act.

1. That payment in priority to all other claims of all claims directed
    by the said Act to be so paid in the distribution of the property
    of a debtor shall be provided for as follows:

    Preferred claims, without interest, will be paid in full in priority
    to all claims of ordinary creditors.

2. That payment of any claims required to be paid pursuant to
    Section 60(1)(1.1) of the Bankruptcy and Insolvency Act shall
    be made as required.

3. That provision for payment of all proper fees and expenses of
    the trustee on and incidental to the proceedings arising out of the
    proposal, accounting fees and consulting fees and legal costs and
    disbursements in connection with the settlement of any dispute
    concerning the amount of any creditor's claim, and in connec-
    tion with preparation of this proposal, including advice to the
    debtor in connection therewith, shall be made in the following
    manner:

    All such fees, expenses, liabilities and obligations shall be paid
    in priority to all claims of creditors

4. That provision for payment of all claims of ordinary unsecured
    creditors, being those persons with claims not referred to in
    Paragraphs 1 and 2 of this proposal, including claims of every
    nature and kind whatsoever, whether due or not due for payment
    as at the date of the proposal, including contingent or unliquidated
    claims arising out of any transaction entered into by the debtor
    prior to the date of this proposal, which creditors shall hereinafter
    be referred to as ordinary creditors, shall be made as follows:

Upon approval being obtained from the creditors and the court, Jack Greene shall pay to the trustee the amount of $500 per month for a period of 48 (forty-eight) months from the date of approval by the court of this proposal, being a total of $24,000.

The amount of $24,000 shall be distributed first to the claimants under paragraphs 1, 2 and 3 above and the balance of funds remaining will be distributed pro rata to all ordinary creditors who have proved claims in the proposal. The creditors shall accept such payments, as payment in full for the debt outstanding.

5. That forthwith after acceptance of this proposal by the requisite majority of creditors, the trustee shall give notice pursuant to Section 149 of the Bankruptcy and Insolvency Act by registered mail to every person with a claim of which the trustee has notice or knowledge but whose claim has not been proved that if such person does not prove his claim within a period of 30 days after the mailing of the notice, the trustee will proceed to declare a final dividend without regard to such person's claim. The dividend referred to in such notice shall be deemed a final dividend and any person so notified who does not prove his claim within said 30 days shall be barred from making a claim in this proposal or sharing in any dividend hereunder, except that a taxing authority may notify the trustee within the 30 days referred to above that it proposes to file a claim as soon as the amount has been ascertained and the time for filing the claim shall thereupon be extended to 90 days.

6. That the creditors may appoint one or more, but not exceeding five, inspectors under this proposal who shall have the powers of inspectors under the Bankruptcy and Insolvency Act.

7. That Mandelbaum Spergel Inc., of the City of Toronto, in the Province of Ontario, shall be the trustee under this proposal.

Dated at Toronto this 15th day of February, 1997.

_____

Jack Greene

144

After filing the proposal, a *notice of proposal to creditors* was mailed to all creditors. Along with the notice, the creditors received a copy of the proposal, Jack's projected cash flow statement and statement of affairs, a proof of claim form (see Case Study 1) and a *voting letter* (a form on which the creditor indicates a vote for or against the proposal). Copies of the notice, statement of affairs and voting letter are shown on pages 145–150.

District of
Division No.
Court No.   31-855992
Estate No. 31-855992

NOTICE OF PROPOSAL TO CREDITORS

IN THE MATTER OF THE PROPOSAL OF

Jack Greene
of the City of Toronto in the Province of Ontario

Take notice that Jack Greene   has lodged with us a proposal under the Bankruptcy and Insolvency Act.

A copy of the proposal, a condensed statement of the debtor's assets and liabilities and a list of the creditors affected by the proposal and whose claims amount to $250.00 or more are enclosed herewith.

A general meeting of the creditors will be held at:
        55 St. Clair Ave. East
        6th Floor
        Toronto

on the 8th day of March 1997 at the hour of 10:00 o'clock in the forenoon.

The creditors or any class of creditors qualified to vote at the meeting may by resolution accept the proposal either as made or as altered or modified at the meeting. If so accepted and if approved by the Court, the proposal is binding on all the creditors or the class of creditors affected.

Proofs of claim, proxies and voting letters intended to be used at the meeting must be lodged with us prior thereto.

Dated at Toronto, Ontario the 16th of February, 1997.

MANDELBAUM SPERGEL INC.
Per:

_____

Trustee

145

District of
Division No.
Court No.   31-855992
Estate No.   31-855992

STATEMENT OF AFFAIRS OF
NON-BUSINESS DEBTOR

IN THE MATTER OF THE PROPOSAL OF
Jack Greene
of the City of Toronto in the Province of Ontario

Type of Assets		Description (be specific)	Exempt property Yes	No	Estimated dollar value
1-Cash on hand					NIL
2-Furniture		Household furniture and effects	X		2000.00
3-Personal Effects		Personal effects	X		1000.00
4-Life Insurance Policies, RRSPs, etc.					NIL
5-Securities					NIL
6-Real Property	House				NIL
	Cottage				NIL
	Land				NIL
7-Motorized Vehicle	Automobile	1989 Audi 5000		X	3000.00
		1996 Taurus (encumb.)	X		10000.00
	Motorcycle				NIL
	Snowmobile				NIL
	Other				NIL
8-Recreational Equipment					NIL
9-Estimated Tax Refund					NIL
10-Other Assets					NIL
		TOTAL			16000.00

February 15, 1997
Date   Debtor

146

STATEMENT OF AFFAIRS (LIABILITIES)

Jack Greene

Creditor	Address	Account No.	Amount of Debt		
			Unsec.	Sec.	Pref.
First Bank of Canada				8000.00	
Best Visa			5000.00		
Canadian Mastercard			5000.00		
First Mortgage Corp.			200000.00		
First Visa			5000.00		
Firstbank of Canada			120000.00		
Firstbank of Canada			100000.00		
Friend A			50000.00		
Friend B			25000.00		
Special Mastercard			3000.00		
Speedy Gas Card			2000.00		
Value Card			5000.00		

Details of Pledged Assets:
First Bank of Canada   -1996 Taurus

TOTAL Pref.	***********	***********	NIL
TOTAL Sec.	***********	8000.00	***********
TOTAL Unsec.	520000.00	***********	***********
GRAND TOTAL			528000.00

February 15, 1997
Date   Debtor

147

STATEMENT OF AFFAIRS

PERTINENT INFORMATION RELATING TO THE AFFAIRS OF A DEBTOR

A- PERSONAL DATA

1-Family Name	Given Names		Date of Birth		
			Day	Mo.	Yr
Greene	Jack		12	09	59

2-Also known as:

3-Complete address including Postal Code
      2 Willow Garden
      Toronto, Ont M3C 4B5

4-Marital Status

  X Married   ___Single   ___Widowed   ___Separated   ___Divorced   ___Common-Law

5-Name of Spouse in full

6-Name of Present Employer	Occupation (Debtor)
Empire Development Corporation	Lawyer

7-Dependents (as defined by the Income Tax Act)

Number aged 15 or less	Number from 16 to 21	Number of adults including spouse
2	0	1

Number of dependents residing with bankrupt (excluding bankrupt): 0

8-Have you operated a business within the last 5 years?	Yes	No	
		X	

B - WITHIN THE 12 MONTHS PRIOR TO THE DATE OF THE INITIAL BANKRUPTCY EVENT, HAVE YOU...

9A- Sold or disposed of any of your assets?	Yes	No	9B- Made payments in excess of regular payments to a creditor?	Yes	No	9C- Had any assets seized by any creditor?	Yes	No
		X			X			X

C - WITHIN FIVE YEARS PRIOR TO THE DATE OF THE INITIAL BANKRUPTCY EVENT, HAVE YOU...

10A-Disposed or transferred any real estate?	Yes	No	10B-Made any gifts to relatives or others in excess of $500?	Yes	No	10C-Made any arrangements to continue to pay any creditor?	Yes	No
		X			X			X

D - BUDGET INFORMATION

11-INCOME		12-EXPENSES	
A Total earnings	5500.00	A Fixed expenses	3000.00
B Contributions of others in the household	NIL	B Others	
		Miscellaneous	350.00
C Other earnings. (Specify)	NIL	Auto Operating Expenses	250.00
		Telephone	75.00
		Clothing	200.00
		Food	400.00
		Car loan payments	250.00

February 15, 1997
Date   Debtor

STATEMENT OF AFFAIRS

PERTINENT INFORMATION RELATING TO THE AFFAIRS OF A DEBTOR

		Meals outside home	150.00
		Heat, light, water	250.00
		Health Club	50.00
		C Payment being made to trustee	500.00
E - TOTAL INCOME	5500.00	F - TOTAL EXPENSES	5475.00

13-Have you been bankrupt before? _____ Yes   X No

14-If you answered Yes to question 13, when did you receive your absolute discharge?

15-Have you ever filed a proposal under the Bankruptcy and Insolvency Act? _____ Yes   X No

16-If you answered Yes to question 15, when did you file the proposal?

17-Give reasons for your financial difficulty.

18-If answers to any of questions 8,9,10,13 and 15 is yes, give details:

   I, the undersigned do swear that this statement is to the best of my knowledge a full, true
and complete statement of my affairs on the 15th day of February 1997 and fully discloses all property of every
description that is in my possession or that may devolve on me in accordance with section 67 of the Act.

Sworn before me at the City of Toronto
in the Province of Ontario
this 15th day of February 1997.

_____   _____
                                                    Debtor

```
District of
Division No.
Court No.   31-855992
Estate No.  31-855992
```

VOTING LETTER
(Paragraphs 51(1)(f) and 66.15(3)(c))

IN THE MATTER OF THE PROPOSAL OF
Jack Greene
of the City of Toronto in the Province of Ontario

I, _____

of _____

a creditor in the above matter for the sum of $_____ ,

hereby request the trustee acting with respect to the proposal to

record   my   vote   FOR/AGAINST   the   acceptance of the proposal

as made on the 15th of February, 1997.

Dated at _____ , _____

this _____ day of _____ , 19____ .

‾‾‾‾‾‾‾‾‾‾‾‾‾‾‾‾‾‾‾‾‾‾‾   ‾‾‾‾‾‾‾‾‾‾‾‾‾‾‾‾‾‾‾‾‾‾‾
Signature of witness   Signature of creditor

‾‾‾‾‾‾‾‾‾‾‾‾‾‾‾‾‾‾‾‾‾‾‾   ‾‾‾‾‾‾‾‾‾‾‾‾‾‾‾‾‾‾‾‾‾‾‾
Signature of witness   Name and Title of Signing
                                    Officer

It was my obligation to explain the proposal to the creditors
and to demonstrate that it was in their best interest to accept
the proposal rather than refuse it, forcing Jack into bankruptcy. I explained in my covering letter that, in a bankruptcy, Jack's house belonged to his wife, and was not
available to his creditors. Even if it had been available, there
was no realizable equity in the home. His car, with equity
of less than $2,000, would be exempt from seizure because
he needed it for his work. As a result, a bankruptcy would
only include the other car and the after-tax value of the
RRSP, as well as some monthly payments for the nine
months of bankruptcy. My estimate of the net money available for creditors, after professional fees, was about $10,000.

The proposal, on the other hand, offered total moneys of $24,000. Even after professional fees and expenses, it would probably result in a distribution of about $20,000 – double the amount available in a bankruptcy. Although the amount was only a small percentage of the total debt, it was all that could realistically be made available to the creditors under the circumstances, and was significantly more than the amount available through a bankruptcy.

A representative from the bank and one personal creditor attended the creditors' meeting. Prior to the meeting, I received voting letters from the other creditors, all voting in favor of the proposal. After a question period, a formal vote was taken. Only the personal creditor for $25,000 voted against the proposal. With the required numbers of creditors and dollars of debt voting in favor, the proposal was accepted.

I then proceeded to have the proposal approved by the court. Jack then provided me with postdated cheques for the 48 months.

THE RESULT

After Jack has fulfilled his obligations and made the final payment, he will receive his certificate of full performance. He will have retained his assets and avoided bankruptcy. And the creditors will receive about ten cents for every dollar owed to them when Jack filed the proposal.

CALL THE AUTHOR

(416) 463-9440

Frank S. Kisluk

PRESIDENT
DEBTOR CONSULTING SERVICES LTD.

VICE-PRESIDENT
MANDELBAUM SPERGEL INC.
TRUSTEE IN BANKRUPTCY

307A Danforth Avenue
Toronto, Ontario M4K 1N7

Fax: (416) 778-6016
E-mail: frank@msg.ca
http://www.debtorconsulting.com